# Smoky

**How a Tiny Yorkshire Terrier Became a World War II American Army Hero, Therapy Dog and Hollywood Star**

by
Jacky Donovan

Smoky's narrative is based on a true story and is as accurate as
practicable based on available reports. With a sprinkling of artistic
licence given that she was, until now, unable to tell her side of the
tale!

# Contents

# Prologue

I can't see. I can't see. There's a hand on my back, guiding me. Gingerly, I step forward. I can hear the crowd fall silent as I feel the first rung. I clamber up. Second rung, third rung, fourth and... up, onto the ledge. Made it.

Oh, of course, you might think that mastering the four steps of a step ladder is an easy feat, but *you* try doing it with a blindfold on. And with hundreds of people watching too.

Now for the wire. I put my head down, sniff and try to make contact with it. There it is. A slight wobble, always a slight wobble then I step out. I am off the stepladder and on the wire. I hear some people in the crowd gasp. I step forward once more. No going back now. I am surrounded by darkness and silence. I move forward. I hear the shuffling of the crowd. I can feel them, willing me on. I keep going. I cannot fall. I will not fall. Onward. Further. Another wobble. Keep going. Moving forward through the dark, cutting through the quiet.

I cannot turn back. I must keep on. I let the wire under my feet guide me. Another step and another. Just a bit further. I feel the safety of the ledge and spring forward. A huge roar. The crowd explodes. The cheers rain down on me. I feel fully charged. I want to jump into the air, run in the fastest, tightest circle I can make.

The blindfold is removed. I am enveloped in light, surrounded by the warm smiles and cries of the crowd. A familiar face beams down at me. "Looks like you did it again. Who'd'a thought a little seven pounder like you would cause such a huge reaction?!"

1

# 1  Running

A whirlwind of darkness and light. It carries me back to ships… and before ships.

But this whirlwind is warm, comforting. Not like the very first one; the real one that led to flying, hospitals and fame. Sorry. I'm running a little ahead of myself. You'll have to forgive lil' ole me for that. I tend to jump around a lot. Or used to.

The first whirlwind. The thunderstorm. Because, if it wasn't for the thunderstorm, I never would have met Bill. I was in the hut when I sensed running outside, so of course I simply had to go take a look. I quickly slipped through the doorway and put my head to the ground. I caught a scent of, I don't know what it was, but I had to follow it to find out. So, down the track I ran, away from the hut and over the hump of grass.

The scent was even stronger now. There it was! Now I could see what I'd smelled. Something small, even smaller than me — and that's saying something — and a dark, dark gray. Four legs and a long tail. It was snuffling around at the ground. If I could only get nearer, I could jump right on top of it. A little closer… Ah, it must have heard me, because it went dashing off. I had to give chase. The game was on. There was no getting away from me. No sirree.

I scampered through the long grass, following the scent all the time. Was that it? Nope. Better keep going. A little further. Gotta keep going. I felt a drop of something on my head that made me twitch. And then another. I hadn't noticed everything around me changing from light to dark gray. Another drop. Two more. I was losing the scent. Keep running. Keep going. I must find it.

Suddenly, gallons and gallons of water tipped down from the skies above. Oh, of course I'd seen the stuff before, but only from indoors where I was warm and safe. I'd never actually been out in it. And the noise! The water poured and poured down, through the trees, bringing huge leaves down with it. It drenched my head and body, forcing me down on the sodden floor. I could barely move, it was coming down so hard and so fast. It was hurting me too.

I managed to crawl over the soaking, muddy ground. There was no scent for me to follow now. I couldn't smell anything. I couldn't see either. I was surrounded by a thick wall of rain. I tried to find some shelter, but it was tumbling down so fast I could barely move. The ground around me turned into small puddles, then bigger puddles as they all joined together.

I had to move. I had to. Slowly, painfully, I crawled on my tummy through the puddles and up into some tall grass. That was better, but not much.

Which way was it back to the safety of the hut? I had no idea. I didn't know if it was back that way, or if I'd find it if I carried on crawling through the long grass. I kept on going forward, one haul at a time. Grass, grass and more grass. I wasn't getting anywhere. I was drenched. I was lost. My body felt so heavy.

Keep going. Must keep going. It was no use. It was getting harder and harder to move through the grass and the pools of water. I finally gave in and whimpered.

Just as I felt that all was lost, the rain stopped as quickly as it had started. The sky changed from gray to blue.

*Where's it gone?*

I heard chattering in the trees, the sound of birds, and the jungle began to turn into life once more. Not me though. I lay there, soaked

4

right through, battered by the rain, lost in the long grass. I closed my eyes. Tired. Drained.

*No! No! Must keep battling on. I must find my way back. I must.*

With heavy, aching legs, I lifted myself up. Teeth gritted, I pushed my way through. When would it ever end? I was moving so slowly, but gradually it got easier. Less and less grass before giving way to a clearing. The ground was still muddy, but I pushed on, through the mist rising from the sodden earth. It was warmer now and I needed a drink. I was so thirsty.

I crawled over to the bottom of a huge tree, its canopy of leaves stretching high, high above. A puddle had formed near its roots. I lapped at the water, but it didn't taste very nice. I wanted to be back in the hut, with my owner. What was she called? My head was spinning. I couldn't remember. The whirlwind was now inside me. Everything was slipping away. Where I lived, who looked after me. What did she call me? I couldn't even remember that. The torrent of water had pummelled everything out of me. What was I going to do now? I was lost, both inside and out.

I was so, so tired. My legs didn't want to move, my head didn't want to work. I lay down close to a thick tree root that was all curled up. I gazed at the root. I could feel my eyes closing, but then… with a hiss and a flicker of a tongue, the tree root suddenly reared up in front of me. I saw the flash of a pair of evil eyes. I had to run, but it was so hard. I leapt up, scrambled around the tree and kept going. Was it coming after me? I was too scared to look around. Go, go, go. My heart was pounding, my head throbbing. Go that way. Keep going. Was that a muddy track? Maybe it would lead me back to everything I knew.

I half ran, half crawled to the track, yet I still didn't know which way to turn. My throat was dry, my head spinning, my back legs didn't want to move at all. I had nothing left to give. I had no idea where I was, who I was or where I was going. I'd even forgotten where I'd come from.

I saw a hole by the side of the track and, with one last push, scrabbled through the mud and tumbled in. I lay there, too exhausted even to pant. My back legs stretched out. My eyes closed. Darkness. I could feel the earth around me. Strangely comforting. My breathing slowed. Where was I? Who was I? It didn't matter. I was just going to stay right there in that hole. Almost safe. A kind of warmth. I lay there for a long, long time, unable to move, unwilling to open my eyes…

\*\*\*\*\*

What was that? My ears pricked up. I'd heard something. A growling. Was something trying to get into the hole? The growling got louder. I felt the earth shake. Louder still. More shaking. It stopped. I heard a bang and a person shouting. I opened my eyes and slowly moved my head. Could I stand up? I put my front legs forward and dragged my body around. If I could only crawl out of the hole.

I edged toward the sunlight. Earth came tumbling in. This was no use. I let out a howl. The shouting stopped. I howled again, louder this time. I tried to creep forward, dragging my back legs behind me. I was moving! I inched closer and closer to where I came tumbling in. My back legs were stinging, but I fought on. I heard another bang and more shouting. Another noise. A truck.

*No, no! Don't go! Don't leave me!*

I crawled forward some more. I was almost at the light now. The sound of the truck cut out. This was it. It had to be it.

I whimpered and howled again. Even louder this time. I was almost out of the hole. I could see the shape of the person. He was standing at the front of the truck, but he turned around. I could see his face, light gray skin. I howled again. Had he heard me? Yes, yes he was walking toward me!

6

*No, not that way! This way! Come closer.*

If only I could pull myself out of the hole.

One more howl.

*That's it. Over here. Down here. Yes!*

A pair of hands, huge and strong, reached down, grasped my body and pulled. I was out of the hole and above the ground in his arms. He was holding me tight. I licked the back of his hand out of sheer joy.

"Well, looka what we got here," he said. "Ah think I've found myself a jungle rat."

## 2  Shaking

The man's eyes met mine. I'd have liked to have said they were warm and friendly, but they looked a little mean and they narrowed as he pored over me. He stretched out his arms and squeezed his fingers even tighter around my sides. I yelped and yelped again as he swung me around and around in the air. What was he doing? Was he about to throw me right back onto the ground? Splat? I shut my eyes, too frightened to think of what might happen next. I felt him move and then drop me... but not back onto the ground.

Slowly blinking my eyes open, I found myself in the back of the truck. Phew! This was better than being in the hole... but not much. I still didn't know what he was planning to do with me.

I heard cursing and a slam coming from outside the truck before my rescuer opened a door and got in. A cough and a slight bang from the truck before it roared back into life and we shot forward. He turned around to look at me.

"So, ah dunno what you are or where you came from, but ah think ah might be able to swap you for some greenback." He sort of smiled, but it wasn't a very nice smile and I didn't understand what he meant. Swap me for what? I knew what 'back' meant but not 'green.' The truck rattled and spluttered and lurched onward as I bounced around in the back, which hurt my aching body even more.

I definitely wasn't what you'd call comfy in there. I was lying on a bag and it was stuffed full, lumpy and hard. It was smelly in there too. A heavy smell, not a nice scent like when I was out in the jungle or running after strange things. It made me cough a little and my head spin, even more than it already was. Where was I going? Where was

9

he taking me? I tried to settle myself, but it was hard because I kept bouncing and bumping around.

Finally, the truck stopped. I heard the door slam and the man came and lifted me out. He held me tightly under his arm as he walked. The sun was beating down, all traces of the storm gone. I looked around, but it wasn't a place I knew. We were in a kind of clearing. I saw some huts and lots and lots of dark tents. I sniffed the air to see if any of it made any sense, but all I got was the smell of lots of men and of food cooking somewhere. Yum.

"Hey, Downey![1] Whaddya got there?" someone called over.

"Ah dunno, Dare,"[2] Downey answered as he walked up to the other man. "Found it in a foxhole when that damn Jeep broke down again. Thass the third time it's done that to me."

The man named Dare looked down at me. I peered back up at him. He had blue eyes, very short hair and a funny little line of hair above his mouth. He looked very young too. Oh, of course, I was at the time as well, but so was he really. A puppy person.

"So what you gonna do with him?" he asked.

*Him? Is he talking about* me?

"Ah'm thinking of the crock pot," Downey chuckled. "Ah could rustle us up a nice bit of stew." I liked the sound of that. I hadn't eaten for a long time.

Dare looked down at me again. *"Anata wa doko kara kita no desu ka?"*[3]

What was that he said?

---

[1] Ed Downey.
[2] Sergeant Dare.
[3] Japanese for "Where do you come from?"

10

*"Eigo o hanasemasu ka?"*[4] Dare continued, laughing.

I was too tired and sore for all this. I had no clue what was going on.

"Well, a Nip ain't had it, that's for certain," Dare offered.

*I'll give* him *a nip!*

"Tell you what, Downey," Dare continued. "Give him to me an' I'll share my chow with you for the next three days. Whaddya say? Better than cooking him up, eh?"

"Done," said Downey, and roughly handed me over to Dare.

I was glad to be free from Downey and even happier I wasn't about to be cooked up, whatever that meant. I'm sure if Downey had anything to do with it, it wasn't going to be very nice. Sure, I was glad he'd pulled me out of the hole, yet there was something about him I really didn't like. I hoped Dare was going to be nicer. He seemed like he might be.

How wrong I was! Before I knew it, Dare had found some hand shears and he began to hack away at all my blonde hair.

*Wait? What are you doing?*

I could feel him pulling and tugging. That was my *hair*. Didn't he know us girls are always mighty proud of our blonde locks? The hair on my head. Gone. Cut. Pull. Cut. Pull. Dare snipped away at all the hair on my back, tummy and then my legs. Oh, of course I know it was all muddy and matted, but I really wanted to keep it. It was mine, all mine. I didn't want him to cut it all off. No sirree.

---

[4] Japanese for "Do you speak English?"

11

I wasn't strong enough to wiggle as he cut and cut. I let out a little yelp, but it was no use. He carried on. I stared at my locks as they lay scattered all around me. I felt just as lost as before.

"Bet you're glad those knots have gone?" Dare smiled. "And you sure won't be as hot."

Hot? Did he think he'd done me a favor? Didn't he know how chilly I felt now, even though it was baking hot? I was shaking from hunger, weak from running and hiding, trembling at the thought of being miles and miles away from everything I knew, which wasn't much at the time. Maybe he was trying to do the right thing though, even if the end result was bad. People do that sometimes. Or maybe he was trying to make my hair as short as his?

"Good boy, eh?" Dare grinned, when he'd finally finished.

*Excuse me?*

He rubbed my head again.

"Good little Smokums."[5]

What was this? Why was he calling me that? Even though I could hardly remember anything any more, I knew this wasn't the place I called home and I certainly knew that wasn't what I'd been called before. I couldn't remember what I *had* been called, but it most definitely wasn't Smokums. What was I *called*?

I wanted to close my eyes and open them and be somewhere else. I used to be a girl dog and now I was a boy dog. Not only that, but I had a totally different name too. What next? What was going to happen to me next? Maybe I didn't even want to know. All I wanted to do was sleep and sleep.

---

[5] The name Dare chose at that time for the dog.

But Dare scooped me up and carried me over to a large tent. We stepped inside, away from the heat and the bright light. It was darker and cooler in there. I tried to stretch my back legs out, but they still really hurt. I wanted to be like I felt before, when I'd run and jump, not like this. I wanted food. I wanted water. I wanted warmth.

"Wass the matter, boy. D'ya want me to set you down? OK," and Dare dropped me onto the floor of the tent. Straight away, I whipped around and tried to run toward the chink of light, but it was no use. I was too slow, as if I was still running through mud.

"Hey, no, little fella. We can't have you running off again," and Dare pressed down on my back, which really hurt. He tied something around my neck which made me choke. I knew I'd had things around my neck before… collars, that's what they were called. But this wasn't a collar. It was much too tight and it didn't feel very nice at all. He fastened a very long cord to the pretend collar and tied the other end of it to a huge wheel lying on the floor.

"Now you can move about a little, but you can't escape." He rubbed my head, perhaps to try and calm me down. Maybe he thought he was doing the right thing again, but I'd never been tied up before. For the second time that day, I gave up. I lay down on the floor. I wanted to run and jump yet, at that moment, lying on the floor was all I could do. I felt trapped. I *was* trapped. I whimpered.

"Settle down, Smokums," Dare said to me, as he stood up. But I didn't want to settle down. And I didn't want to be called Smokums either. I lay there, shaking, frightened, weak.

*The whirlwind is inside and outside.*

Dare turned and walked out of the tent. I was alone. Completely alone. Was this going to be it? Was this going to be my new life now?

## 3  Leaping

I lay there, not knowing what to do. I crawled over to the huge wheel and gave it a sniff. I could smell the earthy scent of the jungle floor. A funny, dark gray bug scurried past me, making a clicking sound as it ran. I tried to bat it with my paw, but it was too fast. I watched as it scuttled off, weaving this way and that, as if it had all the time in the world. Oh, of course the bug didn't know that time and freedom were precious. One moment, I was free, the next I was wet and shaking in a hole. And then there I was tied up in a tent in, well, I just didn't know quite where. I followed the lucky bug's movements as it made toward the light. How I wished I could follow it!

My ears pricked at a noise from outside and the chink of light suddenly widened as two figures stepped inside. It was Dare with another man. They walked toward me, the scurrying bug crushed by Dare under his heavy boot.

"And here he is," Dare said to the man he was with. "Strange little creature."

I had half a mind to growl and bite this new person if they were going to kneel down and touch me. I'd had enough of being prodded and poked, picked up and thrown down, tied up and left, thank you very much.

*Grr! Grr! Snap. Snap!*

I felt another tiny bug run underneath me, but I was much too tired to do anything about it, never mind growl and bite anyone.

"Hey, hey, little thing," said the man as he crouched down in front of me. I lifted my head up slowly to take a look at the owner of this kind voice. He stroked my head softly. "My, you really have been in the wars, haven't you?"

*The wars? I've been in a hole.*

"Who tied him up?" the man glared at Dare. "You?"

"He'd only be escaping," Dare answered.

"How's he gonna do that, Dare? Look at him, he can hardly even move."

This man was right. I couldn't have escaped, even if I'd wanted to.

"He probably won't even make it through the night by the look of him." He untangled some of the cord that had got wrapped around my back legs. He was very gentle though, not like Dare and certainly not like that horrible man, Downey.

"I wonder what kind of dog you are," he said. "I've had plenty of dogs in my time, but I ain't never seen anythin' like you before. Mebbe you're some kind of poodle?"

*A whattle?*

"I love your little button nose," the man continued. "And so small. What are you? 'Bout seven inches tall, I'd say. And look at those beautiful almond eyes."

The way he spoke to me and stroked me was so soft and so gentle.

*I think I like this man.*

"Hey," he turned back to Dare. "What happened to all his fur?"

16

"Ah, that?" Dare smirked. "I cut it off. It was all knotted and tangled up. Thass why I thought I'd call it Smokums, 'cause of the smoky tips it had."

"Well, I've got news for you, Dare," the new man was examining me all over now. "You shouldn't have cut it so much. I bet the color was lovely. 'N' I'll tell you something else for half a nickel as well. This 'it' isn't even a he. She's a girl."

*Finally! Now I like this new man even more.*

"Tell you what, Dare. I'll give you two pounds Australian for her."[6]

"Make it three, Wynne,[7] and she's all yours," Dare replied.

"If she lives through the night, it's a deal," he replied and smacked his palm against Dare's.

Dare left me with the kind man who carried on stroking my head and back very softly. "Hey, girl. You really are so very weak, aren't you? Don't worry, I'll look after you as best I can. You need as much good company as you can possibly get out here."

He didn't need to tell me. No sirree. I licked his hand gratefully.

"Think I'll call you Smoky though. Smokums is such a boys' name, don't you agree? 'N' I'm Bill. Pleased to meet you, Smoky."

Bill? I thought Dare had called him Wynne? But now here I was being given a new name too. First the name I'd forgotten, then Smokums and now Smoky. Maybe that's what people did though? And at least I was back to being a girl. Phew.

---

[6] Approximately $6.44, about ten percent of Bill's pay at the time, so a sizeable fee.

[7] William A. Wynne, born Scranton, Pennsylvania, on March 29, 1922.

"Tell you what, Smoky. I'll leave tied up in here tonight, but I'll go fetch you some food and some water and we'll see how you are in the morning. How about that, eh?"

That sounded divine to me. I licked his hand again and he tapped me on my nose, playfully.

"We'll show 'em what you're made of, Smoky," Bill smiled and stood up. "Three pounds or no."

He left the tent. Although I was still tired and weak, it was the first time since I'd gotten lost that I started to feel better, all thanks to him.

What had he said earlier, about needing as much good company as possible? Well, I knew what that meant. It meant being friends.

*I'm going to be the best little dog I can be. If Bill wants good company, then he can have good company. No more running away for me. No sirree.*

I stretched out on the floor of the tent and waited. My back and back legs still hurt. My tummy and throat too, but that was because I was real thirsty and very hungry I supposed. I heard another noise from outside. It was Bill, carrying two cups.

"Now, I'm not sure what you'll make of this," he said, setting the cups down next to me. "I've got you lots of water to get you through the night and here in this bowl is some Spam."[8]

Spam? Spam. Spam. Spam. I gave it a little sniff before taking a nibble. It tasted better than it sounded. But not much and, at that moment, I didn't really care. I only wanted the horrid, empty feeling

---

[8] Army rations were scant and unpleasant – dehydrated potatoes, powdered milk and eggs, bully beef, vile-tasting mutton, Spam, citric acid, canned fruit, canned tropical butter—which never melted—and coffee.

inside of me to be filled with… with warmth.

*The whirlwind! It's stopped.*

"See you later, my little Smoky." Bill stood up. I gave him a friendly 'yip' in return.

"That's it," he grinned. Then he was gone.

So that's how I met Bill.

His soothing voice and touch helped me forget how much I was hurting. I drifted off to sleep. I awoke to hundreds of ants lining up to join in with the attack on the remains of the Spam in the cup. They seemed to like it more than I did. Something was floating in the cup too, its many legs wiggling as I lapped and lapped, thirsty as anything. I felt much better than I did when I'd fallen asleep though.

Outside the tent, I could hear lots of shouting and the roar of trucks, before I heard something even louder than that. A huge, roaring sound that seemed to buzz right above the tent. The biggest flying bug that I really didn't want to meet.

The tent flap opened and it was Bill again.

"Morning, Smoky," he called cheerily. "How're ya doing today?"

I'd show him how I was doing. I jumped to attention, even though it still hurt a little, my tongue hanging out at one end, my tail wagging at the other.

"Oh, look at your little stubby tail," he chuckled, and I almost turned around to check for myself.

"Come here, girl."

As he came toward me, I leapt straight into his arms.

"Wow. You must be feeling a lot more yourself," he laughed.

What did he mean? I always felt myself, even when I felt bad.

"Are you sure you ain't some springer spaniel?" Bill laughed again. "That was quite some jump there, Smoky, for such a little dog."

He hadn't seen anything yet. When I was strong and free to run around, I'd spring and jump all over the place. As high as a bouncing ball, that was me.

"Come on," he said, finally untying me. "Let's get you outside. I'll make you a better collar too. No running off though."

I didn't need to be told that once. I didn't need telling at all.

I followed Bill out of the tent. My! I'd forgotten how hot and bright it could be. There were lots of other men working in the camp, changing wheels on the trucks, banging hammers against huts, as busy as the ants that'd been snaffling my food. I trotted by Bill's side, happy not to be tied up. I could probably even run and jump a little if I wanted, yet I didn't in case Bill thought I was trying to get away.

A beautiful butterfly fluttered by and almost landed on my nose. It must've thought I was some kind of strange, furry flower. Oh it was so, so pretty! It lazily wafted away and, without thinking, I set off after it.

"Hey! Come back!" Bill called after me.

But I really wanted to chase and catch that butterfly. I was free and hurting less and less.

"Smoky! No!" Bill shouted, louder and angrier this time.

Oh no! What had I said about being the best dog in the world?

Reluctantly, I turned away from the butterfly and trotted back to Bill.

"Good girl," he said and gave me something from his pocket. I don't know what the treat was, but it tasted yummy.

*Must remember not to do that again. Well, the running away part anyway.*

We got to a huge metal box on wheels that was tied to the back of a truck. There was a dark yellow light above the door of the box. When it went off, Bill opened the door and went inside, but I couldn't manage the steps without having to do little jumps.

*One, two three, in we go!*

My nose twitched as the funny smell inside hit me. I didn't know what it was. A man was holding something like a picture up, but it was wet and dripping. He was so busy looking at it, he hadn't even noticed me or Bill.

"Have they turned out, Powell?"[9] Bill asked the man.

"Yes, Wynne, we got some great shots yester— " He stopped when he saw me looking up at him, my little tongue hanging out and my stubby tail all a-wagging.

"Well, blow me. Whatcha got there?" Powell enquired. "That's the smallest, cutest thing I've ever seen."

"This is Smoky," Bill answered. "Downey found her and gave her to Dare. I said I'd buy her off him if she made it through the

---

[9] Captain Powell, in charge of the photo-research unit. Bill was assigned to the 26th Photo Reconnaissance Squadron as a result of attending courses at both Lowery Field, Colorado, and Peterson Field, Colorado Springs.

night."

"Well, it looks like you'll be having to do just that then," Powell smiled. "'Cause she looks mighty fine to me."

I stood up on my hind legs when he said that and they both laughed. No treats this time though.

"Thought I'd find you in here." A voice I recognized. It was Dare, who'd stepped inside the big metal box on wheels. "Looks like you'll be coughing up then, Wynne."

"Sure thing, Dare," Bill replied. "Two pounds wasn't it?"

"I'm sure we said three," Dare answered. "But what the heck. I'm in a good mood and I want to play poker tonight."

Bill handed two small papers to Dare and he pocketed them straight away. He looked so pleased with himself the line of hair above his lip twitched as he smiled. I guessed those little papers were his treats.

"So I suppose you'll be wanting some play time with your new toy, then," Powell said to Bill after Dare had left.

"Well, mebbe," Bill replied. "I wanna show her where she's gonna be sleeping first. No more being tied up for her."

My tail wagged and wagged a lot when he said that.

"Ah, go on," Powell said. "We gotta stack of prints that need to be developed yet though."

"Don't worry," Bill told him. "I'll be working on those till lights out. Thanks, buddy."

Bill went outside and I followed him, spring, spring, spring down

22

the steps.

*I think I might like this new place after all.*

He strolled over to a row of tents under some trees. I saw some holes near them, just like the one I'd hidden in to escape the rain. Bill got to a tent and went inside. I dashed in after him, tail hanging out, tongue wagging. Or was it tail wagging, tongue hanging out? I didn't care. I was happy, happy, happy.

There was a man already inside who sat up from his bed when he saw us. He glared when he saw me and I shrank right back.

Oh no! It was that horrible man, Downey!

# 4 Learning

"Get that out, Wynne," Downey yelled. "I don't want that darn mutt in this tent!"

*Uh-oh.*

I shrank right back against Bill. I thought he would turn right around and get straight out of there, but he stood his ground. He was much braver than me. I wanted to run. Almost.

I looked at Downey and his horrid, screwed up little face, then back at Bill.

Finally, Bill spoke. "She's staying right here," he said, all calm. There must have been something about the way Bill spoke to Downey because, even though Downey still looked angry, he just lay right back onto his bed.

"Well, keep it right away from me then," I heard Downey mutter under his breath.

*Don't you worry, Downey, I won't be going anywhere near you. And, I'm not an 'it' either.*

Bill turned to me. "Just ignore him. Let me make you up a nice little bed and see if we can get you settled." He grabbed what looked like a light gray sheet. "Here, if I fold this up and put it at the end of mine, then you'll be close to me 'n' well away from him. There you go. Good girl."

Bill set me down onto the folded up sheet. It was all snug. Just right for me. If I put my head down, I couldn't see Downey either. So that meant he couldn't see me. Perfect. Well, perfect apart from the heavy scent in there. Now I'd settled down, the stench hit me, as if hundreds of men had slept in there for a long, long time and not even bothered to wash for even longer than that.

Even though I was a girl, I didn't mind getting all dirty and smelly sometimes. I liked to jump around in the mud and splash in puddles of filthy water — who doesn't? — but I didn't want to look dirty and smell bad all the time. No sirree. I didn't know what was worse, being close to someone who didn't want me in there, or being surrounded by that terrible stink.

Even though I wanted to run away from Downey and the lots-of-men smell was really getting up my nose, my new comfy bed must've made me fall asleep, because the next thing I knew was waking up to Bill's soft voice.

"Wake up, Smoky. Wake up. I wanna start putting some meat back on those little bones of yours."

Mmm, meat. I knew what that was, of course, yet the brown stuff in the cup that Bill had given me didn't taste like meat at all. It was even worse than the Spam from before. I chewed and chewed before I finally managed to get it down. I took another mouthful. This mouthful was even harder to get down than the other one. The more I chewed, the drier my mouth became. No matter how much I tried to swallow, I just couldn't seem to do it. Finally, I managed to get some down, but I really didn't want to have any more of that meat again. Not if I could help it. No sirree.

"Hey, Downey," Bill called over to him. "Guess what? She likes mutton."

*I do?*

A grunt. "Who cares? She ain't having any of mine."

26

I had one more, tiny mouthful, more to please Bill than anything, then looked up at him.

"Saving the rest for later, eh, Smoky?" he smiled. "OK. Let's get going." He took my pretend collar off before tying something else around my neck. It felt looser and much better. Then he tied another cord to that and gave it a little tug.

"Thought I might show you around your new home," Bill said. "And then I wanna try something out with you."

Bill put his head out of the tent. Through the gap, I could make out a wall of rain. Bill shrugged. "You'll have to get used to this."

We stepped outside. I could feel him pulling on the cord around my new, slightly better collar. I didn't like the cord at all, but how could I let him know I wasn't going to run off again?

He talked to me as I trotted along by his side, trying to ignore the drip, drip, drip of the water.

"D'ya know where you are Smoky? I bet you don't."

*Of course I don't.*

"We're in Nazdab, New Guinea," he continued. "I wonder how a little dog like you came to be here in the first place. My, how I wish you could talk to me."

So did I. And the first thing I'd say would be to tell him that he could let me go and I wouldn't be running off anywhere. The second thing would be 'can I have a treat?'

"This here is the army camp of the 5212th Photo Wing. We're part of MacArthur's Pacific campaign. 'N' I'll tell you somethin' for nothin'. I'm not even supposed to be here.[10] That's this goddamn war for ya."

Oh, of course, at the time I didn't understand any of what he was saying. War? That word again. Bill had said that to me when he first met me. What was that? All that was going on in my head at the time was what could I do to get him to let me run free.

"But that's jus' the way it is out here," Bill continued. "They take us out. So we have to take them out. Dog eat dog."

*Gulp! I'll have to be real careful if I come across any dogs out here.*

Bill suddenly stopped and looked down at me.

"Mebbe I shouldn't have taken you under my wing," he said. He suddenly looked very serious and a little sad.

"There's been too many good GIs lost out here 'n' I don't wanna see any more lives lost. Especially not yours."

I didn't know what GIs were, but I knew what lost meant, of course, so he needn't worry about that. I wasn't planning on getting lost again any time soon. No sirree. What could I do to cheer Bill up? I quickly decided to get on my back legs again and beg. He'd seemed to like that before. I squatted down and raised my two front paws up to him. Just for show, I stuck my tongue out too. Bill's face burst into a huge smile.

"All right, my girl. I won't let you go." He crouched down and I sprang up into his arms and gave him a nuzzle. Warmth. That really must have done the trick because, when Bill set me down again, he untied the cord from around my collar. Freedom! Immediately, I jumped straight into a puddle.

---

[10] Bill had been working at the American Steel and Wire Works before he was drafted.

The rain stopped. There was a break in the clouds.

"OK, Smoky, I wanna try somethin' now," said Bill, looking up at the sky. "If you're gonna stay here with me and survive out here, then you'll need to learn a few commands. Like all of us."

Bill backed a few steps away from me. I stood there, waiting. What did he want me to do?

"Heel," he said.

I had no clue what that meant.

"Heel," Bill commanded again and pointed to the bottom of his boot.

Why was he showing me the bottom of his boot?

"Heel, Smoky."

Perhaps he just wanted to tell me that part of his boot was called a heel?

One more time. "Come on, Smoky. Heel."

Well, I understood what 'come on' meant, of course. Maybe Bill wanted me to go take a look at the heel of his boot he suddenly seemed to be so interested in?

Slowly, I trotted over and gave his heel a sniff. It had the horrid stench of the tent on it. Urgh. Why would Bill want me to sniff that?

"Good girl," he rubbed the top of my head, got something out of his pocket again and gave it to me.

Yum. The treat was delicious, but the game was puzzling. Was

Bill hoping that I'd get to like the scent? I could tell him a whole heap of smells that were nicer than that.

Bill backed away from me again. "Heel," he repeated and I ran over to his boot once more. Nope. The smell was just as bad. But I did get another treat.

As we carried on playing the heel game and Bill gave me more treats and told me what a good girl I was, I reckoned on this being Bill's way of having some fun. And it was fun. Apart from the smell not getting any better. I didn't think I'd ever get used to it, either on his boot or back in the tent. I guessed us dogs sometimes just had to do things so we could get ourselves a nice little reward.

We played the heel game until the sky above the trees changed from blue to gray and all the bugs in the jungle got louder and louder. By that time, Bill had learnt that he could go very far away from me, shout 'heel' and I'd go dashing straight over to him. Even when it turned gray and I saw some butterflies that weren't very pretty, but I still really wanted to go chase them, I didn't. I just stayed and waited for that word before running over to Bill I'd go.

It was good to see him looking happy again and even better that I'd showed him I wouldn't run off.

"That'll do for today, Smoky." Bill grinned. "I don't want to overdo it."

Didn't he know I could play the heel game until it had gotten even darker? I suppose he didn't. He didn't even know I was trying to start running before he'd even finished saying the word. I wanted to be better and quicker every time. Especially now I was feeling much better. I wanted to show him how fast I could run. I wondered if we'd get to play any more games too. I liked games. If only he had a ball.

We set off walking again, with me by his side. Hurray, he really had learnt! As we got back to the tent, Bill picked me up and examined me all over. What was he looking for?

30

He set me down while he went inside and came back out with his helmet. Why was he bringing his helmet out now? Had he forgotten to put it on earlier?

Bill put it on the ground, but not the way I'd seen the men wearing helmets on their heads.

"In there, Smoky," he commanded with a smile.

The helmet wobbled a bit when I jumped in. I didn't know why he wanted me in there. It wasn't the right way up and it was much too big for me. I sat there, wondering what was about to happen. Bill came out from the tent again with a large container and something else that smelled almost as sweet as some of the strange plants in the jungle.

He poured water from the container all over me. I loved the sudden splash of cold as it hit me. It cooled me down from all the jungle heat. Even when the day was dark gray, it still felt just as warm as when it was bright and sunny. The helmet filled up pretty quickly and some of the water splashed over the sides. Bill started to rub me all over with the smelly stuff. Little bubbles appeared on my body and danced in the water.

"In case you have any ticks,"[11] Bill said to me as he splashed more water on my head and body. "There's danger all around out here."

He washed my head. Suddenly I couldn't hear anything, but with a shake of my head it was OK again.

"You enjoying your bath, Smoky?" Bill laughed, wiping his face.

Yes, I was enjoying it. It felt good as he rubbed my back, underneath my legs, paws and finally my tail. It was wonderful to

---

[11] Scrub typhus, an acute, infectious illness caused by a tick that dogs could carry, presented a serious threat to the soldiers.

feel all fresh and clean, the first time I'd done so for such a long time. I could almost feel my fur springing back to life. Bill poured more water over me until all the dancing bubbles had washed away. I was wet, I was a bit cold, but I was very happy. He lifted me out. I stood there and shook and shook and shook.

Bill laughed again. "Stop it, Smoky! You're giving me a soaking too!"

One more shake and, grr, I felt ready for anything. My fur sprang back up. Oh, why had Dare cut it so short? How I loved my long hair.

Bill crouched down and stroked me. "Right, it's bedtime for you, Smoky and, as soon as you're settled, it's back to the photo trailer for me."

My tail drooped. So he was going to leave me again? Leave me in the tent with the nasty stench and even nastier Downey?

I lay on the floor on the damp ground and looked up at him with pleading eyes.

"Unless you want to come with me, of course?" Bill said.

I sprang up. Wag. Wag. Wag.

Another chuckle from Bill. "All right, let's go."

This was getting better and better. Bill really was learning more and more all the time.

# 5 Training

I was lying in a tray in the metal box on wheels, or the photo lab, as Bill called it. I was wondering why Bill was doing what he was doing when we could both be outside playing. I'd been at the camp for days now and I was liking it more and more, apart from the times when Bill would go off and leave me. The first time that happened, we were in the photo lab when Powell came bursting in. I could tell by the look on Powell's face that it was something real bad.

"It's Hallett.[12] He hasn't returned from his mission."

Bill stopped working and glanced over at Powell, his eyes wide and his voice shaking. "But he was on general reconnaissance in the north sector. There ain't supposed to be any enemy activity up there."

"Yeah, but one shot took him out," Powell said quietly. "McCoy saw it all."

Bill's hands were shaking. "Hallett gone," he said, real angry. "There ain't no mercy out here."

"None at all," Powell replied. "But that means you're gonna have to go airborne now. No more working just on the base for any of us. You're gonna be needed this evenin'."

Bill came over to me and stroked me on the top of my head. He didn't say anything, but he didn't need to. I just knew this wasn't good. For him or me.

---

[12] Captain Sheldon P. Hallett, declared missing in action.

*Uh-oh, the whirlwind's starting up again.*

Whoosh…!

As he left me that night, I watched him walk to his plane and take off, then I stared until I couldn't see it any more. I had to stay in our tent with Downey and all I did was shake. I didn't sleep at all. I just wanted Bill to come back. After I'd cried a little and Downey shouted, "Shut up, mutt," and threw something at me, I couldn't even whimper either.

It felt like the longest night ever. Bill did come back though — I heard his plane before I saw it — and, my! How I wagged my tail and licked his face when I saw him! After that, he would disappear on a mission from time to time and I'd be real sad until he returned. It was then I realized that we both had routines and this was his. Bill went on missions and worked in the photo lab; I played games with him and made him happy. I didn't ever get used to it, though.

I loved being in the photo lab, not only because it meant I could sleep, safe in the knowledge that Bill was there, but I was warm, dry and sheltered from the seemingly endless rain. When we were in there, I'd sometimes watch Bill as he'd gently place a large sheet of paper in a tray full of water, wait for a moment, lift it out and the paper would have a picture on. I'd heard him say once that he wished the pictures were in different colors, but I didn't know what he meant by that. I wondered what different colors were, just like I wondered why didn't *I* change into something else when he dipped *me* in water?

He'd do it again and then again. Bill had told me never to drink the water he used in the trays, but he needn't have worried because it smelled terrible anyway. I liked it in the photo lab. It was very cool and very dark at first. It became less dark after I'd been in there a while, but I was never really sure why that happened.

Sometimes there were other GIs in the lab. I knew what GIs were now. They were Bill's friends and most of them were my friends too.

A lot of them had very short hair like me, although mine was starting to grow back now. They'd all wear the same clothes too, or uniforms as they were called, so the only way I could tell them all apart was by their scent. They'd pass me around and play with me. It didn't take much to make them smile. Sometimes, though, a GI would leave and I wouldn't see him again. Whenever that happened, the other GIs would all stop smiling, at least for a while.

The photo lab was one of my favorite places to be. Another was the place where all the GIs sat at long tables and ate. I think I liked it in there more than they did.

"What's it today then?" I heard Bill ask one of our friends as I sat under a table.

"Steak and corn, hot off the barbecue," was the reply.

Mmm, mmm!

"I swear I'll never touch bully beef again when we get back," Bill said. "Here y'are Smoky… " and a hand would reach under the table where I'd be waiting. Or sometimes I'd walk around underneath the tables, smelling legs and boots to see if I could sniff Bill out. Some GIs would pass scraps of food to me; others didn't, but it was still fun to play.

Another game I played with Bill and some of our friends was running into a hole. The game would start when I heard a really low, rumbling sound, coming from very far away. It would get louder and louder until it was really loud and then all the GIs would stop what they were doing and run and dive into the nearest hole in the ground. There were lots of holes around the camp. Bill would grab me, or I'd run ahead of him and jump right in, just like the time when I was lost. The first few times we played the game, I'd have to wait for the GIs but, after that, as soon as I heard the low rumbling, I'd bark and the game would start a lot sooner. We'd play that game day and night.

But it wasn't what I'd call fun because, just when I thought the growling and rumbling outside the hole couldn't get any louder, it *would* get worse. Much, much worse. The whole ground would shake too, as if all the dogs in the world were jumping and barking at once. I'd be shaking as well. I didn't like it at all. Not at all. No sirree. Bill would squeeze me tight and whisper, "It's OK, Smoky. It's OK." But it wasn't OK. Especially when we'd come out from a hole in the ground and I'd smell a horrible burning smell, much worse than the stink back in the tent, and see flames and trucks that were all broken.

When I wasn't in the photo lab, or playing the food game or the horrible running-into-the-hole game, I'd play much better ones with Bill. After I'd heeled and heeled and heeled, we played a game called 'Sit.' All Bill wanted me to do was sit on my you-know-where when he said the word.

The first time we played it, I looked at the ground and gave it a good ole sniff in case there were any bugs around waiting to sting me, but Bill didn't like it when I did that, so I just had to sit right down and hope for the best. It was a little bit like the heel game, but not quite as much fun because all I had to do was sit there. There wasn't any jumping or running around involved or anything. Sit. Treat. Sit. Treat. Sit. Treat. That was it really, but it sure was a real easy way to get those treats!

Next we played 'Stand, Stay.' Bill would walk very far away from me and call over to me. 'Stand' meant be on all legs. 'Stay' meant not to go anywhere, even when Bill was walking further and further away. Then he'd shout, "Heel," again and I'd go running right over to him to give his boot a sniff.

Sometimes, some of the other GIs would watch as me and Bill played. They'd stand around and laugh and cheer as I'd go shooting over to Bill when he told me to. The more of them that were watching, the faster I'd go. How I loved to hear them all cheer!

"Hey, Wynne," one of them called once. "If I call her to heel, will she come to me?"

38

"Don't even try it, Foster," Bill warned him. "I don't want her getting all confused."

Confused? What did he mean?

One of our best games was called 'Dead dog.' I never was quite sure what a dead dog was. All I knew was how alive it made me feel whenever we played it.

Bill would point his finger at me, shout, "BANG!" and I'd have to fall over on my side and lie there, all still. Bill would come over and poke me in my sides and tummy. Even though it tickled and I wanted to lift my head up and lick his finger, he didn't want me to do that. Instead, he'd pick me up by my back legs and I'd dangle down, my head swinging a little above the ground. At first, I had no idea what the heck he was doing or why he wanted me to be all still. Did he want me to be like that all the time? Didn't he like me any more?

Then Bill would place me on the ground, poke me some more, walk away and I'd wait. "OK!" he'd shout and I'd spring to my feet and dash right over to him as fast as I could go which, by that time, was pretty fast, let me tell you.

However, my most favorite thing ever, what I enjoyed even more than when me and Bill played all those games together, were the times when he'd let me run around completely free. I'd run and run, around and around in circles, getting faster and running in bigger and bigger circles all the time. If I saw a butterfly, I'd run up to it as fast as I could and jump up as it flew above my head before it sailed away. Once, I very nearly managed to get one with my paw. I batted its wing and it landed on the ground but, just as I was about to jump on it, it flew up and was off and away. I'm sure those butterflies enjoyed those chasing games as much as I did.

Other times, I'd run into the jungle. The first time I did it, I was so excited I yapped and yapped. Bill came chasing after me and grabbed me. "Hey, hey, where're you going?" he cried when he finally found me hiding in the long grass. "Don't you know there're pythons around here?"

I didn't know what pythons were — I'd never seen any — but it didn't matter, because it wasn't as if I was going to run away or get lost. Not after last time. Every time I went for a good ole run, I made sure I knew my way back and Bill must have learnt that too because, after a while, he wouldn't call after me so soon. I'd call for him though. I'd bark and yap and play, before setting off to go running straight back, jumping or clambering over tree roots.

Sometimes I'd even chase after the small, fat birds I'd find hiding in the grass. I'd watch them scratching, pecking and cooing. Oh, of course I had no idea what they were saying to each other. They would bunch together and shuffle around, while others would hold their necks up as high as they could, as if they were on watch. They sure did look nervy! Especially when I jumped out from the long grass and chased them. Then they'd all flap and squawk noisily before launching themselves into the air, leaving me a feather or two behind as a gift. They looked and smelled good enough to eat, yet I never did manage to find out if they were.

Just like the butterfly chasing, I did very nearly catch one once. I'd run off to a new part of the jungle, it was still real close to the camp, but the scent was all new to me. As I was about to turn back, I saw a real fat one pecking at the ground. I crouched down and sniffed.

*Mmm. Dinner.*

I ran around a tree and edged closer to the bird. It had no idea I was there. I heard Bill calling me, but there was no way I could yap back, because it would have scared the fat bird away. I moved closer to it. The bird had its back to me and was still far too busy pecking at the ground to notice anything else. I crept even closer to my lovely dinner and was about to launch my attack when something must have startled it, because it flew up and into the branch of the tree above us. How I wished I could fly up into the trees too! Suddenly, it really did feel like I was flying because, from nowhere, someone grabbed me from behind and lifted me right up into the air.

I turned around. I was being clutched by a very tall, very thin, dark yellow person. Another tall, thin, dark yellow person was with him. They looked very different to Bill and the other GIs. They weren't wearing many clothes and their scent was different too. They both started to prod me. Then the one that was holding me lifted me up even higher. Why was he interested in my tummy? I growled, hoping to scare them away, but they both just laughed instead.

I heard Bill shouting my name again and this time I most definitely was going to yap. I yapped and barked as loud as I could.

"Smoky! Smoky!"

Yap. Yap. Grr!

I looked up at the dark yellow, tall man and gave him my best, scariest growl this time. I bared my teeth too, that would scare him. He grinned and showed me his. They were much bigger than mine. Was this a game? I heard a panting sound coming from behind me. It was Bill!

"There you are." Bill came trotting over and smiled at the two men before saying something which I didn't understand. "You pella find my dog?"[13]

The man who was holding me nodded before smiling back at Bill, and not a horrible smile like when Downey had found me either.

"Yessa," the man who was holding me said. "Find dog. Mary dog."[14]

---

[13] Pidgin English.
[14] The word for 'women' in Tok Pisin, the local Creole language in Papua New Guinea, is 'meri.'

41

*What's this? Am I going to be called a different name again?*

Bill laughed. "Yes. She Mary dog."

*But he knows my name. Bill chose my name. Has it been changed?*

The two tall, strange men handed me over to Bill and disappeared into the jungle, although not before I spied the bird above us drop something light gray right onto one of the men's heads. Bill must have seen it too, because he laughed and laughed.

"Well, they do say that's lucky," he roared.

*What on earth is Bill talking about now?*

We set off back to the camp.

"So, you found yourself some natives?" he chuckled.

*Natives? What are they?*

"You've really gotta be careful you know," Bill continued. "I told you there're lots of dangers out here."

I still wasn't sure what Bill meant when he talked about dangers. He cleaned me every day because of ticks, there were the nasty things he'd told me about called pythons and even those natives smiled in a nice way and handed me straight back to Bill. Oh, of course there was Downey and the running-into-the hole game but, most of the time, I was having so much fun I didn't even think about danger. I couldn't feel it or see it or smell it, so maybe there wasn't really any danger out there after all? The only danger I could think of was how easy it was for people to change my name.

"Think we'll do some more training tomorrow," Bill said. "How, d'you feel about that, Smoky?"

Ah. See. No danger at all.

## 6 Falling

Bill was sitting outside our tent. I was on his lap. For once it wasn't raining. It was hot though. Too hot. Out here it was usually mostly raining, often stiflingly hot and sometimes both at once. Bill was holding something. Every so often, with one hand he'd grab a corner of whatever it was he was holding and give it a flick. It made a swishing sound and sometimes the bottom of it would brush against the top of my head. Now and then, he would chuckle, or let out a sigh.

"D'you wish you could read, Smoky?" Bill asked.

*Not really. It doesn't look much fun to me. Not with all the sitting around involved.*

"Hello, what's this?" he suddenly exclaimed. "They're running a contest to find the best mascot in the SWPA[15] region. How d'you fancy being a mascot?"

I didn't want to be a mascot. I was happy being a dog, thank you very much.

"Now, I know you're the best dog there is out here," Bill said, stroking the top of my head, "Whatever type of dog that may be, but how can we show *Yank Down Under* that?"

*Who's* Yank Down Under?

---

[15] South West Pacific Area.

Bill jumped up and I almost fell onto the ground. "I know. I've got an idea. Come on."

He dashed into our tent and came out with our helmet and what I knew to be his camera. I'd watched Bill taking pictures with it around our camp lots of times.

"In your helmet, Smoky," Bill commanded.

I jumped straight in. I'd gotten so good at jumping in that it didn't wobble at all. The sky hadn't gone dark gray yet though, so it couldn't be cleaning time. What *was* he doing?

"Look at me, Smoky. This way. I wanna show them just how small you are."

I poked my head out of the helmet while he clicked away.

"Head up, Smoky. Look proud," Bill called. "Imagine you're on a catwalk."

*Catwalk? Surely he means dogwalk?*

"That's it, Smoky. That's it." Click. Click. "Just one more." Click.

Bill put his camera down on the ground and scratched his head. "Hmm, I wonder if we could do anything else. Something a little more... fun?"

My tail wagged at that word and I jumped out of the helmet.

*Fun? Let me at it! Grrr!*

We wandered over to one of my favorite trees. It wasn't as high as all the others, but it had lots and lots of branches, and vines wrapped around the trunk. Bill stared down at me.

"I wonder if we could... yes, I think we might be able to. Wait there, Smoky. Wait there. Stand. Stay."

Bill sped off and came back with a small, light gray sheet and other things I didn't recognize. Our friends Esmond, Kalt and Barnard[16] were with him too. Esmond was carrying something long that glinted in the sun.

As soon as they got to me, they all greeted me in their different ways — a rub on the head, a tickle under the chin, a cheery, "Hello Smoky." Esmond started to climb up the tree, still holding the shiny thing. I knew something was happening, but I didn't know what. I ran in and out between the legs of Kalt and Barnard, all excited. What was going on?

"No baseball this time, Smoky!" Bill grinned. "Though your paws may leave the ground again." The others all laughed. My you-know-what didn't find it so funny when someone accidentally scooped li'l ole me off the ground, thinking I was the ball when I chased after it one day. No sirree.

I heard a sound I didn't recognize, noise coming from above, within the tree. It lasted for a while before Esmond shouted, "Look out below," and a branch came crashing down.

*What's he doing to my favorite tree?*

Bill spread the light gray sheet out onto the ground. More and more branches came falling down around us. We all moved further away so we wouldn't get hit. Barnard was unfolding a thick blanket. Kalt had Bill's camera. What *were* they doing?

Esmond clambered down the tree and came over to join us. "That should give her enough clearance," he grinned and rubbed my head again. Bill and Barnard each held a corner of the blanket. "Yeah,"

---

[16] Don Esmond, Howard Kalt and John Barnard.

Bill said. "That should do it. Come here, Smoky."

I trotted over, obedient as ever. He set the blanket down and grabbed the small sheet. Cord was attached to some of the edges of it and a collar connected the other ends of the cords together. "Put this on, Smoky."

We hadn't played this game before. I didn't know what on earth he wanted me to do. He took my front legs and put the large collar around me. It went right past my neck and around my body. Then Bill pulled it tight.

"Are we ready?" Bill said to everyone. They all nodded. I didn't nod of course. I didn't know what we were getting ready for. Bill lifted me up and handed me over to Esmond.

"Ready for action," Bill grinned.

"Come on, Smoky," Esmond said. I looked at Bill. He didn't usually let me follow his friends' orders.

"Go, Smoky," Bill patted me on the head. "You'll be just fine."

*Whatever he says... Here I go...*

Esmond tucked me under his arm and ran back over to the tree. He jumped up, grabbed a branch and hauled us both up. He stood on the branch and reached up for the next one. He was so fast, he was like the little screeching and chattering furry puppy men I'd seen swinging in the trees. It really did feel like I was flying up in the trees to catch a bird — just like I'd wanted to when those natives found me.

Higher and higher we went. I didn't dare look down. Bill said I'd be fine, but it sure didn't feel fine to me.

"Hang in there, Smoky, not far now," Esmond whispered to me

as we climbed.

Another branch and another, until finally we stopped. I peered out from under his arm. My, how small Bill and the others were! As small as me! Esmond sat down on an overhanging branch and held me in his lap with both hands.

"Here we are, Smoky, how's that? Safe as houses up here," he reassured me as I sat there, shaking. I saw Bill and Barnard looking up at us, each holding a corner of the blanket stretched out between them.

"All right, Esmond!" Bill shouted up to us. "Let her go!"

Esmond held me out at arm's length, high, high above Bill and Barnard. I scrabbled and scrabbled with my back legs.

*No! No! What are you doing?*

"OK, Smoky," I heard Esmond call. "One, two, three. Jump!"

And he dropped me, right out of the tree. I shut my eyes. The whirlwind was in my tummy, turning it upside down.

*This is going to hurt!*

Thud! I plopped into the blanket that Bill and Barnard were holding and everyone cheered. My heart was thumping hard.

Kalt coughed. "Er, you'll have to do it again. I didn't get it."

I wasn't sure if I *wanted* to do it again. I felt as if my tummy was still up in the trees somewhere. I barked at Bill.

"Oh, I'm sorry, Smoky," Bill said while I was lying on the blanket on the ground, trying to get my breath back. "I forgot to give you a treat, didn't I? There you are."

The delicious treat made me feel much better. Esmond joined us.

"Back up you go," Bill laughed and Esmond and me set off again. This time I looked up when Esmond let me go. I caught sight of the light gray sheet above my head open up and waft in the breeze. The thought of another treat made it a bit more enjoyable this time, not that I had much time to think. Another thud. Bill and Barnard caught me in the blanket again, then set me down on the ground. I was still shaking all over, but it felt like the sense of fear was now being chased out of me by a sense of fun.

"D'you want to do it again, Smoky?" Bill asked after he gave me another treat.

"I'd say she does," Barnard pointed at me. "Look at her. She's having a whale of a time."

If whale meant very strange then, yes, I was. Esmond lifted me off the blanket and dashed over to the tree. Up we both went. He sat on the same branch and dropped me again. This time, I really did enjoy it. Wheee! This was a great game!

On the fourth time, I managed to look all the way down. Bill and Barnard quickly got bigger and bigger and then they vanished as they caught hold of me and I became buried in the softness of the blanket. The fifth time we did it, I even managed to bark too. This was getting better and better.

"OK, guys. Let's make the next one the last one," Bill said to everyone.

*Aww shucks. Just when it's getting real fun.*

"Whaddya say, Kalt?" Bill continued.

"Sure thing, Wynne," Kalt answered. "One more, and then we've got it in the bag."

I didn't want to be in a bag. I wanted to be back up there in the tree. I wanted to fly.

Esmond grabbed me and hauled me up the tree for the final time. We got to the branch and he sat down. He held me out. Last time.

*Here we go...*

As Esmond let me go, I felt a strong breeze knock me sideways.

Whoosh...!

I just had enough time to look down, but now Bill and Barnard weren't underneath me with the blanket. They were to one side and there wasn't enough time for them to shuffle across and cat—

Cccrunch!

Ow! Ow! That really hurt. I'd landed — splat! — onto the ground. I think I even bounced like a ball. I yelped. I couldn't breathe.

*My back! My back!*

I felt Bill's hands on me and heard him cry, "Oh, Smoky! Smoky! I'm so sorry, that was so stupid of me." I felt his thumbs digging into my back.

*Yes, there. Right there.*

We must have both heard the crack, because Bill said, "I think you'd maybe dislocated something. How does that feel, Smoky?"

I don't know what Bill had done but, after that cracking sound, I felt *much* better. I turned around and gave his hand a lick.

*Surely I deserve lots and lots more treats for this?*

# 7  Balancing

This was more like it!

The firm earth felt good under my you-know-what as I sat watching Bill. We were outside our tent. Bill was doing something with two stepladders as I watched from inside the shadow the tent made. The shadow was one of my favorite places to sit. It was a little cooler than in the blazing sun. He attached two wires to the stepladders. They dragged on the ground until he moved one of the stepladders further away and the wires sprang up tight. Bill stood back, coughed and wiped his brow.

"Whatcha doin' there, Wynne?" Dare asked as he walked past. "Ain't you heard we're all getting shipped out to Biak soon?"[17]

"Jus' you wait 'n' see, Dare. Jus' you wait and see," Bill replied and coughed again.

Bill turned to me. "Are you ready for this, Smoky?"

I wasn't sure. After Bill's last idea of a fun game that involved me being thrown clean out of the tree and hurting my back, I wasn't sure I wanted to do anything that might involve danger again.

He attached a leash to my collar, lifted me up and sat me on top of one of the stepladders. I looked across at the other stepladder, at

---

[17] Biak Island dominates the entrance to Geelvink Bay, near the western end of New Guinea. It was held by 11,000 Japanese troops under the command of Colonel Kuzume Naoyuki. It was vital that the airfields there be taken in order for the army to move swiftly to the Philippines.

the wires running between them both, then back at Bill.

"Now, Smoky, d'you reckon you can make it from one stepladder to the other?"

*Ah, well, if that's all he wants me to do — easy!*

I turned to run down the steps and then across to the other stepladder. Bill laughed, coughed, picked me up and turned me back around.

"No, I mean walking on the wires," he chuckled. "Don't worry, I can use the leash to help you balance. No falling this time. I promise."

I looked at the wires swaying in the wind, high, high above the ground. All right, maybe I'm exaggerating a little bit, but have *you* ever tried walking on wires?

Bill tugged on the leash a little. "Go on, Smoky. I'll help you."

Was he crazy? How was I going to get from over here to over there? I'd never realized just how much I loved walking on the ground. I looked at him, but he just smiled back.

I swallowed. I thought of the treats he'd give me.

*Here we go again!*

I put one paw gingerly onto one of the wires, then another. My paws were pretty tough, but it still felt strange. Uncomfortable. And not what my paws were designed to do, for sure. I shuffled forward, even though my you-know-what really wanted to stay put. I felt Bill's hand on my back.

"OK, just a step further, Smoky, and then you'll be balancing."

Sometimes Bill seemed to know what I was capable of much

more than me. So, if he thought I could do it, then I'd really try my hardest to do this balancing, whatever that meant.

I stepped forward again, then my back legs left the stepladder and found the wires too. I so wanted to look around, but Bill said I had to keep looking ahead.

*Keep going! Must keep going!*

I carefully moved my paws again. Whoosh…! Was that a wobble? Did my tummy flip just then? Bill steadied me.

"It's all right, Smoky, I can lift you off if you don't like it."

I didn't like it or not like it. But I didn't want Bill to lift me off. Not just yet.

I kept moving forward. Front leg, back leg, front leg, back leg. Then I heard Bill calling me. I looked up and saw him at the other stepladder. I panicked a little as I realized he no longer had his hand on my back.

"Come on, Smoky, come on. You're past the middle now. Not much further."

I pushed on. I thought of how I'd escaped from the tree root, of how I'd fallen and missed the blanket. If I could do those things, then I could do this. Bill knew. Front leg, back leg, front leg.

*Not much further now. A little more.*

"Come on," Bill called out and coughed.

Back leg, front leg, back leg, a slight jump forward and — yes! — I reached the other stepladder. That was such fun! Bill clapped before putting his hand in his pocket. "Here you go, Smoky. Well done!" I happily gobbled down my treat while Bill tickled my ears, laughing.

Dare walked past again and looked at us both. "What've I missed?"

I don't know what I enjoyed more that day — walking up and down the wires, getting faster and faster, watching the other stepladder get closer and closer, or when I walked across when it was real dark. Yes, after I'd done it again and again without even falling to the ground once, Bill stopped and scratched his head.

"Tell you what, Smoky. Let's try somethin' that's never been done before. Somethin' to really show folks just how great you are."

He tied something around my eyes.

*What are you doing? I can't see anything!*

"How's the blindfold feel, Smoky?" he asked.

I felt like I couldn't see, but that was because I couldn't see. Everything was darkness. I wondered what I looked like too. I hoped the blindfold wasn't messing my fur up. I'd had such a lovely brush that day!

"Go on, Smoky, just one step," Bill continued. "I'm sure you can do it."

*He really has gone crazy!* I wasn't sure if I could even walk on the ground without being able to see where I put my paws, never mind balancing in the air. My heart was beating so fast, I was certain I'd fall off those high wires. But, for Bill, I'd give it a try. It turned out that feeling the wires under my paws meant there was only one way I could go. It helped that I could hear Bill too, even when all I could see was darkness. Front leg, back leg, front leg again. Yet I didn't wobble.

"Come on, Smoky. Come on, you're doing so well. Nearly there!"

I kept going and going until I felt the stepladder underneath my paws, a last jump and — I'd done it! Phew! Bill took the blindfold from my eyes. I blinked in the sunlight and caught sight of Bill's happy face. Another treat for me.

I loved all the games me and Bill played. I even loved the being-thrown-out-of-a-tree game until I missed the blanket and hurt my back, but running across the wires, and especially running across without even being able to see them, was the most fun of all. It was like running across the ground, only up in the air. A different kind of flying. I wanted to do it again!

# 8  Pining

After our game had finished, we went to where the GIs ate, hopefully to play one of my other favorite games too. I scampered on ahead of Bill. It was funny to feel the ground all solid beneath my paws. Bill was moving very slowly. He kept wiping his dripping wet face with the back of his hand. He moved so sluggishly and was coughing so much, it was all he could do to keep up with me and my little ole legs.

That night, I was woken up by a strange and horrible noise — a sound I'd never heard before. It was Bill whimpering. I jumped up onto his bed and tried to lick his face, but he brushed me away. What was happening?

Downey woke up too. "Get off him, you mutt. Wynne! Wynne! Can you hear me?"

Bill moaned.

"You gotta be ship shape for the Biak assault," Downey continued. "You know if we don't take them out there'll be no advancing to the Philippines."

But Bill simply moaned again and croaked: "Water, I need… "

"You need more than water, buddy," Downey said. "I'll go get a medic."

He pulled on his boots and dashed out. What was going on? It must be something bad if Downey was trying to help.

He came back with someone I hadn't seen before. He knelt down next to Bill, wiped the top of Bill's head and wrapped his fingers around the bottom of his arm.

"His pulse is racing," the man said to Downey. "And, judging by those sweats, I'd say we've got another case of malaria."

"Dunno what's worse out here," Downey muttered gruffly. "The Japs or the mosquitoes."

The man turned back to Bill. "Wynne. Wynne. Can you hear me?"

Bill nodded his head slowly.

"We'll get you to 3rd Field.[18] You can rest up there for a few days."

Bill groaned.

"Well, ah ain't lookin' after him while Wynne's in hospital," Downey snapped and pointed at me.

"Petril— Fran— Frank," Bill mumbled.

"Yeah. Petrilak," Downey nodded. "He can have him. Come on, mutt, let's go. Take care of yourself, Wynne."

I really didn't want to leave him. I took one last look at my poor ole Bill before following Downey out of his tent and trotting slowly behind. What was happening now? Where was Bill going? Today had been so much fun and now it had suddenly changed to... to what?

We got to Petrilak's tent and Downey poked his head in. "Here, Petrilak," I heard him say. "Visitor for you," and Downey grabbed

---

[18] A Nazdab hospital for injured troops, consisting only of very basic tents.

me and threw me into the tent.

*Ouch! Watch what you're doing.*

The smell in there was even worse than the one in my and Bill's tent.

"Wassa? Wass goin' on?" Petrilak sat up from his bed. It was dark in there but, as I got closer to him, I could just about make out his scent from the really horrible one. I recognized it from playing the will-they-won't-they-give-me-scraps-of-food game. He was one of the ones that always did, so at least I knew I'd be getting fed.

*I wonder if he'll clean me and play games with me too? Sure hope so.*

It wouldn't be as good as being with Bill, but at least it would be better than staying with Downey.

"Oh, hey, Smoky," Petrilak[19] said, lying back. "What you doin' in here? Where's Wynne?"

I had no clue. I just knew I wasn't with Bill. He had something called malaria, but he didn't have me. My tail drooped. I didn't know what to do. I just stood there. I could make Petrilak out now. He had a line of hair above his mouth like Dare's, but no hair at all on his head. He looked a bit like the ball I'd been running after earlier.

He patted his bed. "Well, I dunno how or where you sleep with Wynne, but jump up, Smoky, jump up."

That made me feel a little better. But not much. I sprang up and landed on his legs. Petrilak reached his hand out and I gave it a lick.

"Just hope you don't have malaria too," Petrilak said quietly.

---

[19] Frank Petrilak.

61

I wasn't so sure. If it meant being with Bill, then I would choose having it over not having it every single time.

I didn't see Bill for days and days after that. Oh, of course, Petrilak fed me and took me for walks around the camp, but it didn't feel the same without Bill. Where was he? What was happening to him? Petrilak must have noticed I was looking real unhappy because, after more days and days had passed, he and Kalt put me in the back of a truck and I went for another bumpy ride. I didn't mind this time though. In fact, I was real excited about it. We were off to see Bill in the hospital. Petrilak had said so. We might not be in the camp, but at least we'd be back together.

When I got there and Kalt lifted me out of the truck, the familiar scent hit me. I hadn't been to 3rd Field before, but I definitely recognized that clean smell. Just where had I smelled it before? Maybe it was just because I'd been sleeping in hundreds of smelly men tents for such a long time that this sparkling scent made my nose tingle? Nope. It tingled inside my head too. It was definitely something else.

A smiling man — a medic he was called — took us through a huge tent and opened a curtain. Bill was lying in bed. My Bill! His face had changed from light gray to yellow, but he looked much better than before.

"Hey, you two," he grinned, when he saw Kalt and Petrilak. "And Smoky! My! I'm surprised they let you in here." My tail thumped and thumped against Kalt.

*Put me down! Put me down!*

Bill sat up, reached out his arms and I jumped straight into them. I licked his face all over.

"Have you missed me, eh?" he laughed. "I've missed you!"

"It's only been three days," Kalt chuckled. "How you doin'? You look... weird."

"They've been pumpin' me with Atrabine,"[20] Bill replied. "So don't go mistakin' me for the enemy. Speakin' of which. Any news?"

Petrilak and Kalt both sat by the side of Bill's bed.

"They're shippin' us out to Biak," Kalt answered. "How long you got in here?"

"Few more days I reckon," Bill said as he stroked me under my chin. "Turns out I got a dose of dengue, not malaria. Still sucks though."

"Yeah," Petrilak and Kalt both nodded. "Here, I got somethin' for ya," Petrilak said after a short pause and threw something at Bill. "Addressed to you."

"Hold on a mo', Smoky." Bill opened whatever it was and pulled something out. "Copy of *Yank Down Under* magazine, and, hello, what's this?"

He opened the magazine. I watched his eyes move from side to side and then down, before his face burst into a huge smile.

"Wow! Smoky, you've won first prize in the mascot contest. First prize! We did it!"[21]

Kalt and Petrilak shouted, "Yesss!" I didn't know why, but I decided to join in as I was just so happy to be with Bill again. I barked and yipped until the medic who'd brought us to Bill's bed stuck his head through the curtain.

---

[20] Used to treat malaria, Atrabine temporarily turned the skin yellow.
[21] Smoky won an engraved silver cup while Bill received a free copy of the magazine for a year.

"Keep it down, guys, I got some of ya buddies out here and they're pretty nervy."

"Ah, sorry 'bout that, Ray," Bill said. "'S just that my little Smoky here's won first prize in a Yank comp and we got pretty excited about it. We'll keep it down."

"I knew I shouldn't have let a dog in." Ray shook his head as he replied, but I could see he was smiling. "Well done, Smoky."

I was happy to have made everyone so happy, but I wish I knew what I'd done.

Kalt and Petrilak left shortly after that. Not me though. Ray came back in and said that, seeing as I'd cheered Bill up so much, I could stay until he was better and ready to leave. That made *me* feel even better too.

"D'ya mind if I take your Smoky to visit some of the other guys in the ward?" Ray asked Bill later that day. "I think he might be of some comfort."

"Sure, if it's OK with Smoky, go ahead," Bill looked at me, then handed me over to Ray. "He's a girl, though."

"Even better," Ray grinned.

I wondered if I might see some of our other friends in there. I knew they'd fuss over me and give me treats.

We went through the curtain and walked down rows and rows of identical beds. Some of the men had sheets tied around their heads or arms, others were sleeping or hidden under the covers completely. What was this place? Why did it feel so... so sad? We stopped at a bed in the corner. Someone was sitting up in it, but he didn't move his head to look when Ray settled us both on the chair.

64

"Got a visitor for ya, Jack," Ray said to the man when he finally turned to us. Jack didn't smile when he saw me though. In fact, he didn't seem to see me at all. It was as if he was looking at something very far away. Slowly, Jack lifted his arm up, reached out and placed his hand on my back. Ray lifted me off his lap and sat me on the bed. I could feel Jack's legs underneath me. He didn't take his arm off me as Ray moved me. He just let it rest there on my back while I got comfy. That's when I noticed that the man's other arm was missing.

*Where's his arm? What's happened to this poor man?*

I wanted to run right back to Bill.

"I'll leave you here for a few moments," Ray whispered and left us both alone.

*No, no. I don't know what's going on. What can I do to help him?*

I really wanted to jump off this man's bed then, but something about him, the fact he just looked so unhappy, also made me want to stay. I knew what unhappiness felt like. I lay there and let him rest his hand on my back.

We stayed like that for a long time. He didn't make a sound and neither did I. I looked up at Jack's face — another puppy person — as he closed his eyes. I saw his bottom lip tremble. A drop of water appeared in the corner of one eye. It shone before rolling slowly down his cheek, dropping onto his chest and vanishing.

I don't know what he saw when he closed his eyes. Maybe he'd been lying in a hole in the damp earth too?

# 9  Jumping

The small but nasty-looking hairy puppy person was baring its teeth at me. It looked like it was about to jump on me again. I'd seen ones like it swinging up in the trees, but never this close before. I'd thought they were friendly, but this one wasn't at all. No sirree. Colonel Turbo,[22] he was called, and he belonged to a Sergeant Bice I'd met when me and Bill arrived here. The place was called Biak, but it wasn't somewhere I would have called home.

I was confused. I didn't know where my home was any more. I'd thought the army camp in Nazdab was to be my home but, after I'd spent time with all those poor men in their beds and the hospital let Bill go, we upped and left as soon as we got back to the camp. At the time, I didn't know why some of them had arms or legs missing, why some of them cried and shouted while others didn't say anything. I didn't know why those men in the hospital all seemed to be very far away, as if they were lost and trying to find something. Now I knew.

If being lost meant staying in strange places and diving into holes in the ground, if it meant going on missions and coming back with arms and legs missing, or not coming back at all, then no wonder a lot of them seemed lost.

Now here I was, not exactly lost, but here with Bill in this strange new camp. All I knew was that we kept moving because it was something to do with this thing called 'war.' I couldn't see it or smell it, but I knew it was all around us somehow. The GIs must have known too. They reminded me of the fat birds I used to chase.

---

[22] A rhesus monkey, mascot of the 25th Photo Reconnaissance Squadron and runner-up in the *Yank Down Under* competition Smoky won.

Wherever we went, they seemed to bunch up all together, a few with their necks all stiff, looking out and around the camp, while the others seemed to twitch and cluck, all nervy.

And everywhere we went, I couldn't escape from the endless heat, the endless rain and the bugs that always seemed to find me. Even the food was always the same. If it wasn't for Bill and his treats and our games I don't know what I would have done.

Colonel Turbo lunged at me, but I jumped out of his way just in time. Maybe he was just playing a game with me but, to me, this didn't feel like a fun game at all. And sorry if you feel I'm jumping around a lot with my story here, but it is such a big story for such a little dog. And I did tell you I like to jump around!

Even though my new home felt strange, at least I knew who I was. Back in the 3rd Field hospital, Ray had introduced me as 'Smoky Champion Mascot of the SWPA.' I didn't know why my name had got longer, and Bill still called me Smoky, yet it seemed to make everyone happy when they heard me called that. Just as we were leaving the camp in Nazdab, Kalt showed something to Bill that made him even happier too.

"Here y'are, Wynne," Kalt said when he handed it to Bill. "Copy of *National Geographic*.[23] There's somethin' in there ya might like to see."

Bill's eyes opened real wide when he read it.

"Well, darn me. Here's a picture of a dog that looks just like you, Smoky. You're a Yorkshire Terrier. And what a mighty fine specimen you are."

So, from then on, I knew what I was too. Not only was I Smoky, but I was a Yorkshire Terrier and the mascot of the whole SWPA region. I wasn't quite sure what it meant to be a mascot, but I knew

---

[23] April 1944 edition.

it must have meant something to the GIs because, no matter where I went, they all wanted to hold me and ask Bill lots of questions about me.

"How d'you feel owning a famous dog, Wynne… what sort is he?"

"Smoky here's a Yorkshire Terrier," Bill would say proudly. "I never knew what breed Smoky was until I came across it in *National Geographic*. Been in England since the 1860s, they have. Bred to go catch rats in mines. And he's a she too by the way."

And, for the moment, I also knew where I was. I was here, in a small army camp called Biak, and I was being attacked by this crazy looking Colonel Turbo. I bared my teeth at Turbo and he backed away, but I knew it wasn't enough to make him stop.

This was the first time I'd been under attack and I didn't like it. When we left Nazdab, Bill said it could be dangerous and we'd have to be on the lookout for the enemy. Those words again. Maybe Turbo was my enemy? He was definitely a real danger to me. But why wasn't Sergeant Bice trying to stop him?

Me, Bill and some of the others had left Nazdab in a plane. I'd watched the planes take off and land at the camp — and I'd heard them, of course — but I hadn't been in one before. I didn't know what to expect. It was like being back in a truck but much, much louder and it moved much faster. My tummy felt like it did when Esmond flung me out of the tree. I didn't know what was shaking more, me or the plane itself. It was cold too.

I didn't know what was happening. It was only when Bill lifted me up to a small, round window and I could look down and see the tops of trees getting smaller and smaller that I realized we were up in the air. I was flying! Really flying. Just like the birds I chased, only this was much higher, much faster — and much louder — than them!

We landed in a place called the Admiralties. The camp was much smaller than the one in Nazdab and there were lots of men I didn't recognize. They greeted me and Bill like old friends though. Lots of them seemed to know who I was, or they'd call me 'Yankee Dog' and rub my head. They made me feel very welcome, not like this horrible Colonel Turbo, who made me feel like I wasn't wanted at all.

I didn't stay in the Admiralties too long. Bill gave me to a man called Bishop[24] and we flew off in his plane, leaving Bill behind. I didn't know why we'd left Nazdab for the Admiralties and I didn't know why I was moving on again either. All I knew was that Bill was staying behind to go on more missions and I didn't like that at all. Our friends went on missions and some of them didn't come back. What would happen if Bill didn't come back?

That plane was even more frightening than the first one, and the journey even worse without Bill. The plane was much smaller, made a lot of noise and shook and shook. Bill had told me not to worry and that he'd join me later, but I did worry. I didn't know where I was going, or why he was staying behind. I trusted him, but I still didn't like it that he sent me off without him. He said he had some important work to do, but what could be more important than looking after me?

Bishop handed me over to Barnard when we eventually landed in yet another strange place. I was real glad to escape from his shaky little plane and it was good to see and be with someone whose scent I recognized.

While I stayed with Barnard and pined and waited for Bill, I made friends with a lovely dog called Duke.[25] Oh, of course Duke wasn't a patch on Bill, but he had big, soft, brown eyes and a wet nose. My tummy sure did turn and turn when I saw him, as if I'd eaten some butterflies and they were all fluttering around inside me. We played lots of fun games too. I wasn't quite sure what one of our games was called. All I know was that it was real fun, but real quick.

---

[24] Lieutenant William Bishop.
[25] A mixed-breed terrier.

So it was good to be with friends old and new. Barnard and Duke were definitely my friends, while this Turbo — who was rushing forward to attack me once more — was definitely my enemy. Turbo lunged at me again, grabbed my front legs and pulled me to the ground. I could feel his horrible little arm pushing down on top of me, my tummy lurching, my throat dry.

*Stop hitting me! This game's no fun.*

I managed to shake myself loose from his clutches and I growled at him, but I knew that wasn't enough to keep him away for long.

The camp where I waited for Bill was called Hollandia, but I didn't know that until Bill finally, finally appeared.

"How're you liking Hollandia, Smoky? Have you missed me?" he grinned as soon as he saw me. I jumped right into his arms, my tail wagging. My! How glad was I to see Bill again!

Oh sure, Barnard fed me and let me run around, just like Petrilak did when Bill was poorly, but it wasn't the same as being with Bill. How I wished we were both back in Nazdab. We spent a lot more time together there.

In Hollandia, there were plenty of times when Bill would leave me with Barnard because he had to go on a mission. I was always scared when he told me that. Real scared. Every time Bill disappeared, I'd stay very close to Barnard, or just lie down and wait for him to return.

"Don't fret, Smoky," Barnard would try to reassure me. "He'll be OK." But it was never OK. Not really. How did Barnard know that Bill would be OK? Even Bill never knew if our friends were going to come back. What if Bill didn't come back at all?

And, when he did, we'd go straight into the photo lab and stay in there for a real long time. He'd work and work. Dipping papers, turning them into pictures, hanging them up to dry. I'd sit there and watch him. Why was he working so hard?[26]

And why did Turbo still think this was fun? He was running at me again, snarling, about to attack.

Just when I'd thought this was all Bill and me would be doing — him working, me watching him work — we'd uprooted yet again except, this time, the place we went to was much better. It was called Brisbane[27] and, instead of it being rows of hot tents in the jungle, it was streets and buildings and clean.

And the food. My! Fresh meat, Bill said it was, and it was much, much better than the stuff out of tins he'd been feeding me the past few months. I also had lots and lots of something delicious to drink too. Milk it was called and it was divine. But what made Brisbane even better, was that Bill wasn't working at all. All we did was eat and drink and play. All the other GIs we met were happier too, they smiled much more than the ones that were sleeping in smelly, stuffy tents back in the jungle.

It was real swell to walk down a street alongside Bill. People would stop and talk to us, or they would bend down and stroke me. They all marveled at my hair, which was now lovely and long again. I felt like a real girl for the first time in such a long time. Bill had even bought me a brand new blanket. Even though it was very hot when it was bright, I was shiveringly cold when it was dark. The blanket was lovely and very warm and snug. Bill said it was green, but it looked gray to me. Maybe he sees different things to me.[28] We went to a place called the Red Cross and the people there put lots of little pictures on my blanket.

---

[26] The photo lab worked round the clock, eventually — in September 1994 — receiving a Presidential Unit Citation as a result of the photographic coverage of the Philippines it provided during September 1944.
[27] Bad weather grounded the planes and Bill and colleagues were given rest leave.
[28] Dogs see on a different color spectrum to humans.

"Look what they've done for you, Smoky," Bill exclaimed when we went to collect it. "You've got a 5th Air Force patch, corporal's stripes, a US insignia, two six months overseas bars and wow, lookee here, an Asiatic Pacific ribbon and a good conduct ribbon too." Not for the first time, I had no clue what he was talking about. All I knew was that the blanket was lovely and warm and it was mine.

And if I had that blanket with me, I would have thrown it right over Turbo, bundled him up in it and sat on top of him. He grabbed my nose.

*Ouch! When is this so-called game going to stop?*

While we spent our days relaxing in glorious Brisbane, we went to see a man at *Yank Down Under*. He gave us a funny silver cup with two handles and everybody got excited as Bill took lots of photographs of me wearing my blanket, my paws on the cup. I'd've rather had a treat really, but the cup seemed to make Bill and his friends smile a lot.

We visited another hospital while we were in Brisbane too. This one was called the 109th Fleet Naval Hospital. It was much bigger than the one Bill had been in, and in a big ole building too. But, just like the other hospital, it had that strange scent that tickled my nose and my head. What *was* that scent?

As well as GIs, there were marines and sailors in there. They still all looked the same to me though, all sad and broken, with missing arms or legs, or covered up in what must have been their blankets. Some of the GIs were in chairs on wheels. They would follow me and Bill around as we went from ward to ward, asking if they could hold me. Bill would always let them, he said it was good for something called morale — whatever that was. It was good for me too, because they'd feed me tidbits.

After a while, I'd hoped that Brisbane was going to be our new home. I loved playing the games that Bill had taught me for all the poorly GIs in the hospital. On Bill's command, I would heel or sit, play dead or howl along to a song. We also played a game called 'The Grapevine' where I'd run through and around Bill's legs as he quickly walked along. I don't know who loved that more: me, Bill or the GIs.

But Brisbane wasn't our new home. Instead, we flew in another plane and landed here in Biak and I didn't like it. I didn't like it when we were sleeping in the tent and the horrible, wailing noise started — sounding like the loudest, saddest dog in the world — and me, Bill and all the others had to run as fast as we could into a cave. And I really didn't like being attacked by Turbo. No sirree.

This was it. Just like those poor GIs in the hospital, I was going to do my best to see off this enemy, no matter what it took. I had to make it stop. I batted his horrid, clawed hand off my face. Then I lunged at him, bit him on the nose and jumped on top of him. Turbo looked shocked, screeched and ran off.

I'd done it!

I'd defeated the enemy![29]

---

[29] Bill and his colleagues were delighted to see someone finally take on Turbo and win.

## 10 Rolling

"Come on, Smoky," Bill was pointing. "You can do it!"

We'd been in Biak for a long time. Whenever Bill disappeared and came back, he said we were making advances on the enemy. I didn't know what that meant. All I knew was that, for a while now, I didn't want to jump or run around so much. I didn't know why. I felt hot. I felt tired. I felt... fat.

So, at times like this, even though it was much better being with Bill and playing with him than when he was away on one of his many missions, I didn't know if I wanted to play, if I even could play. Sometimes, just sometimes, all I really wanted to do was lie in the shadows and escape from the hot sun, or chase those magical butterflies. Most of the time, a rub of the head, some kind words or a treat from Bill would help. I'd spring up and jump or sit and wait for his command but, every so often, I'd find it real hard.

"Come on, Smoky," Bill cried again. Up you go!"

Running and jumping on the ground? Walking in the air on wires, sometimes when I couldn't even see? Oh of course, I could play both those games, and I was good at them too, but this, this was something else. When I walked or ran, the ground underneath me didn't move. When I walked on the wires, apart from a little wobble sometimes, the wires didn't move either. But walking on something that moved too? Well, I really wasn't sure I could do that. No sirree. Especially when I was feeling so doggone tired and so... full.

Bill had tipped a huge oil drum on its side and was rolling it along the ground, like a big, wide wheel going around and around. Was this like one of the games that Bill sometimes wanted me to play but I found real hard? Like the shape game? Ever since he'd asked me if I wanted to read, from time to time Bill would point at some strange shapes that he'd cut out of paper and say, "Find 'S' Smoky," or, "Where's 'M'?" I never had a clue what he wanted me to do though, so I'd just run over and give the shapes a sniff.

"Never mind, Smoky," he'd say and tickle me under the chin. "Maybe even a wonder dog like you can't do everything."

So was this one of those times? Could I jump up onto a rolling oil drum? Wouldn't I just fall off? It was real high and moving real fast. OK, maybe I'm exaggerating a little again.

"Go on, girl," Bill said. I looked at him. Then back at the oil drum. I thought of the other games I'd played with Bill that I never thought I'd be able to do. I thought of that nasty Colonel Turbo.

*If I can beat a nasty hairy puppy person, then I can beat this. OK. I'm gonna try it. I'm gonna give it a real good go.*

I stood up, took a few steps backward, ran a little way and — spring! — I jumped up and landed right on top of the moving oil drum.

*Oh no! I'm going to fall!*

I scrabbled and scrabbled, my feet on the barrel. I could feel it moving underneath me, could hear my nails against the metal. I felt as if I was going backward and, if I moved my legs too fast, I felt as if I was going to tumble over. Bill kept turning and turning the drum around and around. It was much harder than running on the ground. I had to find my balance, just like when I was walking in the air on the wires.

After what seemed like a long time, and my legs were nearly worn out, Bill commanded, "OK, Smoky, jump down."

I leapt off the moving oil barrel and landed back on the ground. I had to take a step forward because, after all that running on the drum, it felt as if the ground was moving too. I sat down, tired, panting.

*Why am I so out of breath?*

I looked up at Bill.

"How d'you like that, Smoky?" Bill grinned. "I knew you could do it."

I had a treat and some rest, then Bill started to roll the oil drum along the ground again. I took a deep breath, stretched out my back legs and, with another jump, landed on top of it… and instantly rolled right off. I landed on my you-know-what and yipped out of surprise and frustration.

"Let's keep going," Bill chuckled, after checking to make sure I was OK. "Unless you don't want to do it of course."

I did want to do it again, even though I felt real heavy. I barked and wagged my tail to let Bill know.

"That's my girl. You *can* teach old dogs new tricks after all!"

*Hey! I'm not old!*

I made sure not to fall off the next time. Jump and up, around and around, scrabble and scrabble. There! If I kept my head up, I was able to do it without slipping off.

We played that oil drum game all day. Even when it was real hot and I was panting, I wanted to do it more and more. By the time it got dark, I could run, jump and stay on it, even when Bill was making the oil drum roll real fast. It still felt like the ground was moving, though, every time I jumped off though. Or maybe I was still moving?

Something was happening to me, but I didn't know what. I lay down on my side, my tongue hanging out, breathing fast.

Bill's voice. Concerned. "Hey, hey, you OK, Smoky? What's up?"

But I was too tired to yip. I closed my eyes, but then I felt myself just wanting to push. I pushed and pushed and...

"Well, I'll be damned!" Bill cried.

I stopped pushing and turned my head around to look behind me. There, all glistening and tiny... was the treat I'd gotten from playing that game with Duke! I must have won then!

Whoosh...!

Bill wasn't there when I woke up, but Petrilak, our tent mate, was. As was my prize — Topper,[30] he was called, and divine doesn't even come close to describing him. All black and cute as can be. So, while Bill was on another mission, and even though it made me worry, I now had another worry too. Something else to care about.

Me and Bill had been sharing a tent with Petrilak since we'd arrived in Biak. Oh well, Petrilak would just have to get used to sharing his tent with another. It was much better than sleeping in a tent with Downey. I hadn't even seen *him* since me and Bill left Nazdab. I wasn't sure what had happened to him.

So it was another day spent waiting and worrying, wondering where Bill was. I stayed with Topper all day, in between pacing around, my head down, tail drooping, waiting for Bill.

---

[30] Named by Petrilak who adopted him.

"Whatcha doin' there, Petrilak? And how've they both been?"

*It's Bill. He's safe!*

Petrilak stopped what he was doing.

"Just another letter back home. I got some this mornin'. How 'bout you, Bill? You told Margie[31] yet about your other woman?"

"I'll write when I have time," Bill answered, solemnly. "Jus' been out with 3rd Emergency Rescue to see if we could find a downed pilot."

"And did you find anythin'?" asked a GI called Crays,[32] who was sitting with us.

"Yeah. Lots of Jap foxholes and a P38 with the cockpit ripped off. The poor guy wouldn't have had a chance." Bill had a faraway look in his eyes, the kind I'd seen on the men's faces in the hospital.

"Did you get fired at?" Petrilak said, his eyes all wide.

"Luckily, no. The lieutenant from 3rd Emergency told me the foxholes had all had hand grenades dropped on 'em on a mission yesterday."

Nobody spoke for a while or even looked at each other.

"Tell you what, Wynne," Crays looked at me and Bill. "If you get knocked off, you gonna let me have Smoky?"

Bill glared at him.

"No chance, Crays. She's gonna be goin' with me from now on.

---

[31] Bill's girlfriend, Margaret R. Roberts.
[32] Jack Crays.

If I go down, then we both go down together."

I didn't much like the sound of either of those things. I wouldn't want to be looked after by Crays — for one thing, he smelled real different to Bill. And, even though I loved being with Bill all the time, I didn't much like the sound of us both going down together. Something told me that didn't sound at all good. No sirree.

I found out what going down together might mean the very next day. And I was right. A GI called Bardsley[33] had been sent on a flying mission over somewhere called Ambon, but not returned. I was with Bill when Crays told him about it. I knew Bardsley, he was a good friend of Bill's and he was nice to me too. I also knew what missions were, of course, they were the danger that Bill talked about and what it meant when someone didn't come back from them. That's why I was always sad when I knew Bill was going on a mission.

But here we were both going on one together. Was that better or worse? I didn't know. We left Topper behind with Petrilak. I gave Topper a nuzzle while Bill was examining a bag I hadn't seen before. Then we trotted over to the small airfield. Just as we were about to board the plane with some other GIs, Bill crouched down, unzipped the bag and gave the command for me to jump in. I looked at him, puzzled.

"C'mon Smoky, it's the only way. You'll be safe in here."

Hesitantly, I jumped right in. I could barely see out of the top of it.

"What've you got there?" One of the GIs called over to Bill as he made sure I was comfy inside the bag.

"It's Smoky. Squadron Mascot," Bill answered. "She's coming with me."

---

[33] Lieutenant Clair J. Bardsley.

"Maybe she'll be our lucky charm," the GI smiled a thin smile. "And if—"

He was interrupted by one of the other men.

"OK, guys. The equipment's loaded and you're all good to go. Remember, if you take a hit, try to aim for a coastline landing if you can. Those jungle villagers don't like outsiders. Some of the crew from 90th Bomb Group came down in Ambon and you know what happened to them."

One of the other GIs — Bill said he was the navigator — nodded. "Yeah. Dinner."[34]

Dinner? Which reminded me, as we all climbed up and into the huge plane — I was real hungry. Bill had said he didn't want to feed me if we were flying in case it made my tummy turn, but he needn't have worried about that. My tummy turned anyway as we rumbled along and then lurched up into the air. Bill hung me up in the bag at the front of the plane. I could feel my whole body swing backward as we went up and up. I could have looked out of the window if I'd wanted to, but I just closed my eyes and waited for my tummy to get back inside my body.

It didn't though. The skies outside the plane got darker, from dark gray to real dark gray. The plane rolled and dipped, dropped and dipped some more, and I felt as if I were falling out of the tree and slipping off the oil drum at the same time. I shrank back into the bag, trembling.

I hoped I'd hear someone shout, "There he is, there's Bardsley!" but the shout never came. Not that I could have heard any shouting anyway, because it was so, so noisy in the bag, in that lurching plane. It dropped and shook, rose a little and then dropped again. My whole body shook, my ears hurt a bit from all the noise. I didn't like it. I wanted to be back on the ground with Bill.

---

[34] Eaten by a tribe in Dutch New Guinea.

We flew on for what seemed like days and days. Eventually though we must have turned back. The plane got lower and lower and was shaking less and less. We landed with a bump that nearly threw me right out of the bag.

*Phew! We've landed! We've made it!*

But I knew that meant Bardsley hadn't made it. I'd never seen Bill looking so sad before. We'd got back safely to the camp in Biak, yet Bardsley hadn't. That meant that Bill had lost a real good friend. I stayed by him extra close those next few days. We didn't play any games. Bill was just real quiet, so I made sure I didn't jump or run around as much. I still licked his hand though. And his sad face.

"See what I mean about losing good friends out here?" Bill said as I sat in his lap. "And it isn't over yet."

He was right. We went on lots more missions after that. Sometimes when the sky was light gray, sometimes when it was dark gray. Sometimes we were in a plane for a long time, other times we were up there for a real long time. Even when I was wrapped in my blanket in my bag, it was always cold and it was always real noisy. And even though I would pant and shake, I was still happy to be with Bill. I would think of me and Bill playing and wait until we were back on the solid ground again.

Bill always had his camera with him. But it wasn't fun like the time when he took pictures of me sat in his helmet. No sirree. I didn't always know what we were doing either. I just knew it had something to do with war, the thing I couldn't see yet always seemed to be around us, hiding, waiting to pounce, just like that curled-up tree root that attacked me once. Or Turbo.

I didn't know which was better — to be threatened by a horrid, hairy puppy person, which at least I could see, or to forever feel under attack by this thing called war, which I couldn't see at all. But as bad as all the flying was, one thing I knew was that at least it couldn't get any worse.

## 11 Barking

We were on the move again but, much to my relief, we wouldn't be flying. This time we were going by ship, whatever that was. I guessed it'd be a whole heap more fun than being in a plane though. Bill told me that ships went over water, rather than moving in the air.

"So now we can test your sea legs too, as well as your air legs. See if they're better than mine," he'd grinned. I didn't know what air legs or sea legs were, all I knew about were furry legs, like mine.

But even though going on a ship sounded like a whole heap of fun, I wasn't sure if I wanted to be on the move again. I loved being in the camp in Biak. I had Bill, Petrilak and the others, but I also had Duke and now Topper too. He really was getting quite big — well, big for a very small dog anyway. And, even better, Colonel Turbo wasn't there any more either. Sergeant Bice had gone off with him somewhere and he came back alone.

"Did you do it?" Petrilak asked him.

Sergeant Bice nodded. "Had to. He was causing far too much trouble for everyone."[35]

*You're telling me.*

Just before we set off, something happened to my head and tummy again. I don't know what it was, it was as if I was tumbling

---

[35] The monkey's viciousness escalated and, after biting his keeper badly, it was decided he would have to be shot. He was deemed too dangerous around people, but without the jungle skills to survive if set free.

and spinning, but in a good way not in a scared way. It felt like the butterflies in my tummy when I saw Duke, or the tummy flip when I was learning to walk on wires, not the wobbly tummy I had on the flying missions. It was strange. It was just like when I'd been in the hospitals and smelled the scent of, of… something.

The GIs were all sitting around tables eating the most delicious-smelling food when it happened. I was on Bill's lap, as usual, and everyone was feeding me lots of lovely tidbits.

"Here y'are, Smoky, try this. Turkey."

I nibbled a slice of the light gray meat and then more and more. Yum!

"Here," another called over. "Why not try some pumpkin pie or cranberry sauce?" he laughed.

Bill smiled too and stroked the top of my head.

"Happy Christmas," he said.

*Happy what?*

I don't know why but, as soon as Bill said that, I stood straight up and yapped and yapped right in his face.

"What's the matter, Smoky?" Bill asked. "All I said was Happy Christmas. You are happy, aren't you?"

That word again.

I barked and barked. That's when my tummy started turning, my head spinning. A whirlwind of happy, happy, happy…

And my head was still spinning when we left in a truck a few days later. Where were we heading off to? Why did I jump up and bark when Bill said that to me? It felt like something I didn't even have to think about, just like when I wanted to run and chase after butterflies.

I was still so confused with everything. Staying somewhere, moving on, shaking in planes, jumping off oil drums and still feeling as if the ground was moving even when it wasn't. I couldn't wait to be on the ship. Surely, whatever a ship was, it wouldn't move around as much as I felt I was doing. Whenever I closed my eyes, I saw Downey or Bardsley, Turbo or a GI with no arms or legs. When I opened them though, I saw Bill, and then everything slowed down. And that was all I needed.

"This is it, Smoky," Bill whispered. "We're on our way to smoke out the Japs. Next stop. The Philippines."

When the truck finally stopped moving, I could smell a change in the air. The lush jungle and the scent of grass gave way to a vast expanse of water — the biggest puddle I'd ever seen. Such a fresh, salty smell. And so blue! I felt the breeze ruffle my hair. My locks must've looked lovely in the breeze. I sure was ready for my entrance!

Bill lifted me out of the truck and set me down on the ground. It was hot, soft and crumbly. I tried to run, but my paws kept sinking into it. I watched as lots of other trucks drove along a bridge into what must be the ship on the giant blue puddle. I could see men on it waving and hear them calling.

I had to get back into the truck, because it was cooler in there and the ground was starting to burn my paws. We sat and waited a real long time. I gazed at huge pale gray birds with big yellow beaks, riding on the wind on their long flying arms. I couldn't wait to get out and give chase. Eventually, we rolled forward. I heard a clank as the front of the truck lifted up onto the bridge, crawled forward and then right into the ship itself. It changed from blazing hot sunshine into lovely, cool darkness.

The truck stopped.

*Can I get out now? I'd really like to explore.*

"Hang on there, Smoky. It'll be safer for you in here while we load up." Bill said to me. "Stay."

*Awww. Shucks.*

I waited and listened. I heard lots of banging and a lot of men shouting. It didn't smell so fresh any more. It smelled of the inside of the truck, only much, much stronger. I waited, panting a little, for Bill to come and get me out.

I heard him whistling before I saw him standing outside the truck. "OK, Smoky. Let's show you around."

I stood up, slowly. I sure needed some water.

Bill lifted me up and carried me out of the truck. I saw lots of other trucks had driven onto the ship, all lined up and filling the whole room. We climbed a flight of stairs. I could hear his boots clanging on the steps. We walked quickly until we came to the edge of the ship. Again it smelled so fresh out here and — my! — I looked down at the huge shining puddle rushing underneath us, stretched out all around. I couldn't see where the blue of the sky melted into the blue of the puddle.

"How d'you like the sea, Smoky?" Bill asked. I could feel my ears flapping backward in the breeze. "Come on, let's get some chow." As we walked back inside the ship, Bill put me down and I sniffed my way along the strange metal floor. He walked through a door and I followed him. The noise and smell hit me right away. It was a bright, long room with lots of men sitting at rows of tables. Could I play my favorite game here?

I spied Petrilak and Cray sitting in a row along a table with lots of others. Duke and Topper were there too. When I wasn't cleaning

Topper or showing him how to be a dog, Petrilak looked after him, just like Bill looked after me.

"OK, stay close to me," Bill said. "We'll eat and then I'll show you where we're gonna be sleepin'."

We walked over to where Petrilak and Cray were sitting.

"Mind if I join you?" Bill asked, squeezing in next to a GI I didn't recognize. He smelled real nice though.

"Sure thing," he replied. "I'm Wilson. Which squadron are you from? And where did you find such an adorable creature?"

Wilson reached down to me. I grabbed whatever it was in his hand. I'd hoped the food on this ship would be better than back in the camp, but it wasn't. If anything, it was even worse. It was drier and even harder to chew.

"Next stop, Luzon," Petrilak smiled between mouthfuls of food.

I wondered where that was and how long it would take to get there, never mind why we were going there in the first place.

"If we even make it," Bill replied softly.

Gulp. "If I go down, then we both go down together," I remembered him saying.

As I watched Bill and the others eating, I picked out a scent I truly didn't recognize — not food, not this strange ship, not lots of smelly men. Then I saw it. It headed toward me. It was large, had four long, long legs, dark gray spots on its light gray body and its nose in the air.

As it got closer, it eyeballed me and snarled.

Uh-oh!

"Who are you? What are you doing on here?" It asked and tried to sniff my you-know-what. Finally it stopped growling.

"I'm Smoky," I said. "And I don't know what I'm doing on here." I really wanted to not sound scared. But I was scared stiff.

"Well, this is a war ship, so it's gonna be pretty darned scary, so you betta be tougher than you look. I'm Major," he said. "And you look kinda cute, so pleased to meet you."

I breathed a sigh of relief.

*I think I've made a four-legged friend.*

"Stop whining, you two," Bill looked down at us both. "Time to hit the sack, Smoky. Let's go."

I gave Major a quick sniff before setting off after Bill.

We walked out and down and along and around until we came to a narrow room with lots of beds hanging up.

"This is ours, Smoky," Bill pointed at a swinging bed. "Up you get, though maybe we might sleep on deck sometimes. Nicer for you."

I jumped up, the bed rocking a little as I did. As I lay there, the bed didn't stop rocking. Not even when Bill had clambered in and more and more GIs got into their beds. As I lay there trying to sleep, I could feel the ship rolling from side to side. I could hear a howling too. Was that Major?

Nope. The howling was definitely coming from outside the ship and it was getting even louder. The ship rocked to the side again and I got the tummy feeling again, as if I was falling sideways.

92

More howling, more rocking. Bill sat up.

"Think we might be heading into a typhoon. No sleep for us."

"Sick bags at the ready," I heard someone call, and all the GIs in the beds groaned.

The ship started to rock even more. Now it seemed to be going up into the air too, before crashing back down. Sideways. More winds. Whoosh…! Up. Down.

*Where's my tummy?*

Bill was holding onto me. "I said we'd test your sea legs," he grinned, but his face was a real light gray when he said it.

The howling got even louder. Up. Down. This way. That way. I heard some men coughing real loud before smelling a horrid smell.

*Uurgh!*

Bill held onto me even tighter. He must have heard me panting.

"Hold on there, Smoky. Hold on."

But I had nothing to hold onto. I dug my claws into the bed and rocked and panted. I wanted to bark, but my throat was so dry.

The boat lifted up once more. I waited for the lurch. It lifted higher and higher each time, and each time I waited for the lurch. Yep. Bill was right. There really was going to be no sleep for any of us.

\*\*\*\*\*

We'd made it! Somehow, some way, we made it through to the

93

morning each day. The howling and rocking had lasted for days and days. I was still panting and shaking, my fur all knotted and tangled.

"Must be all the salty air," Bill said as he gave me a much-needed morning brush. "Well done for making it through, Smoky."

I was real hungry, yet didn't want to eat. I still didn't really know where my tummy was. Back in the room of rows of tables, though, Bill gave me something and I managed to chew, swallow and get it down. Somehow it found my tummy.

"Boy, that was a rough one," he said to Petrilak.

"I don't think we've seen anythin' yet," Petrilak replied, solemnly.

He was right. I hadn't seen anything. I'd heard it though and felt it of course — my, had I felt it! And that was more than enough for me.

Later that day, Bill showed me more of the ship. It was so huge to me, I didn't know how Bill was able to find his way around. After we'd eaten some more horrid meat that came out of cans and Bill was sitting at a table playing a not-much-fun-looking game called cards, I smelled and saw Major trotting toward us.

"Did you enjoy the typhoon?"

"No, I didn't. It sure was horrible."

And then! All the dogs in the world howled at once. The biggest whirlwind of all. "Incoming! Incoming! All army personnel below deck!"

Bill sprang to his feet, grabbing me and running out of the room. Major was following close behind us, his tail dragging on the floor.

"Batten down the hatches!"

I barked and barked. I had no clue what was going on.

*Where's Topper? Where's Topper?*

"Sshh. Not now, Smoky!" Bill said firmly.

We were crouching down with some others. I heard the whistling sound coming from outside the ship.

*What's that?*

The whistling got louder and louder until it was almost as loud as the howling of the typhoon.

*Please don't let it be another typhoon.*

Men were sitting real still, tense, waiting, but waiting for what? The whistling got louder still. It made my ears hurt. Bill put his hands over them.

"Open fire!" I heard someone shout. "He's getting closer!"

And then it got even noisier. The ship bounced and rattled.

*What's happening? What's happening?*

I looked up at Bill. He was trying to see what was going on too. It was so loud. It was so scary.

TAKA-TAKA-TAKA-TAKA-TAKA!

The whistling turned into a screech and then a huge boom. The whole ship rolled.

"Kamikaze. Down!"

I heard cheers. But this was nothing to cheer about. I wished we were back in the typhoon. I wished we were back in the tent with Downey. Even being attacked by Turbo. Anywhere but here. Anything but this. I turned around and could see Major cowering behind us.

Another whistling sound and the ship rattled again.

TAKA-TAKA-TAKA-TAKA!

The screeching sound again. Louder and louder. I waited for the boom. It didn't come. But the screeching got even louder.

BOOM!

The whole ship burst into noise and heat. I saw fire, heard men screaming. Bill's hands were still around me, holding me tight.

"Medic! Medic!" I heard someone crying. Wailing.

Boots ran past me and Bill. I started to cough. It was getting real dark and filling with thick, choking smoke.

"Think we need to get out of here!" Bill started to crawl along the metal floor. Through the smoke, I could just about make out Petrilak clutching Topper. I heard Duke too. Phew! I looked down at the shapes all around me and Bill, then I realized they were bodies, all smeared in something that looked sticky. Bill stepped over one of them. He lifted me up onto his shoulder, so I could see behind us as we crawled forward. I could just about make out a light gray lump with dark gray lumps, stretched out on the floor. Four legs. Not moving. I heard more screaming, could smell the horrible burning smell, my eyes stinging.

Finally, I knew. I knew what war was.[36]

---

[36] Bill and Smoky were fortunate to survive, a shell missing them by only a couple of inches. Over 200 kamikaze planes had attacked an assault force the previous day and a total of 24 ships were sunk and 67 damaged. It had been the largest Naval Force ever gathered, with over 170,000 troops involved.

# 12 Swallowing

We'd made it to the Philippines[37] — those of us who'd survived the journey and made it off the boat, anyway. Through sheer good luck, we hadn't been attacked again as we'd journeyed on, but I still couldn't wait to get off and be back on dry land, real land that didn't move. It was beyond horrible to see Major and those men lying still, covered in sticky stuff, some with bits of them missing. The thing I hadn't seen, yet was all around me, I finally saw.

*Do I look lost now? Like the wounded men I saw in hospital?*

I definitely saw the sadness in Bill's eyes, so I tried to be as good a friend to him as it was possible to be. I kept closer to him, I played all our games as best as I could, jumping higher, running faster, moving even more quickly across the wires and on the oil drum. I didn't know if we'd get to play any more of those games again when we first arrived. I didn't know what to expect.

*What if those who attacked us on the ship are lying in wait?*

I did see them, as it turned out. Our enemy. The Japanese. But they were all caught behind a big wire fence. A prisoner of war camp, Bill said it was called. They didn't look nasty though, like Turbo. They just looked real sad and oh, so very thin. I didn't know whether to feel sorry for them; whether I should feel sorry for them. I saw mounds of rubble too. Bill said they used to be buildings. As we traveled to our new home, huge trucks with long noses rumbled past us and I saw hundreds of GIs all working — making things, fixing

---

[37] They set up camp in Lingayen on the island of Luzon, approximately 140 miles northwest of Manila.

things.

Me, Bill and the others didn't stay in tents at first. The people who lived in the village let us stay in their strange-looking houses. I don't know where they stayed or where they went to. They were even thinner than the prisoners of war I saw[38] and desperate to help the GIs clean things, mend things and make things. Then they'd wait around for scraps of food. It didn't seem like a game to them, though.

I'd never seen houses like theirs, made from bamboo Bill said — even the stepladder we had to clamber up to get inside. My paws would slip down the gaps in between the bamboo when I walked around. After a while though, me, Bill and the other GIs moved back into tents. They were much bigger than the ones back in Nazdab or Biak. This time we shared our tent with Barnard and some GIs we'd met called Graham, Tankersly and Kuzmicki.[39]

They dug a shelter in the crumbly ground too. I knew what that was for — so we'd have somewhere to hide if I heard the rumbling, growling sound coming from very far away. I sure wasn't looking forward to playing that game again. But I helped them as much as I could.

"Out of the way you crazy mutt!" Kuzmichi shouted to me, laughing. So I jumped around, ran some more and dug a little harder.

Whenever I heard the scary rumbling of enemy planes, I'd try to grab my tail between my teeth and then keep trying to grab it. Bill always said it was real useful when I did that. I just couldn't help it. I did it, but didn't know why. And, anyway, 'Chase tail! Chase tail!' was less scary than 'Plane coming! Plane coming.'

On one of the days that the planes didn't come, I'd just finished playing a game called tug of war with Barnard and the others. I sat panting alongside Bill. It was a real hot day and, for once, Bill wasn't

---

[38] The Japanese had taken whatever food they could find when they passed through.
[39] John Graham, Jack Tankersly, Alan Zzumicki.

100

working either. We were playing the shape game. Again! Bill had spread them out on the ground in front of me.

"Come on, Smoky, come on! I bet you can do it if you really try. Once more. Where's 'S'?"

I stared at the shape. I was still staring at it when I smelled someone. I glanced around and saw Gapp[40] walking toward us. Gapp was my friend. He sometimes worked with Bill too.

"Hey, Bill?"

Bill peered up at him. "Yeah? I'm not on yet, am I?"

Gapp smiled. "No. But we've got a problem down at the airstrip. We need to put some telephone lines under the runway. Trouble is, if we take up the steel matting, dig up the runway and put it all back, it'll take days. Which means the planes'll have to be diverted."

"Well, I'd love to help you guys out," Bill answered. "But my field is taking photos, not brawn."

Gapp laughed. "Thanks for the offer, but I was thinkin' more Smoky here. The thing is, the pipes for the wires are sixty foot long and a little more than eight inches wide."

Bill looked surprised. "You mean—"

"Yeah," Gapp interrupted. "I saw a cat in a newsreel do it in Alaska. They blocked him in so he couldn't back out and blasted him through with compressed air."

*Gulp.*

"Well, I ain't sure about the compressed air," Bill laughed.

---

[40] Sergeant Bob Gapp.

"Don't think she'll wanna be blasted through like a rocket."

*My hero.*

"You know the war's ended in Europe?" Gapp stared at Bill, all solemn.

Bill nodded.

"Well, I dunno how long we're still gonna be out here for," Gapp continued. "But I sure think doing this might just make that time come a little sooner."[41]

Bill nodded again. "OK. Let's give it a go. Whaddya think, Smoky?"

*Double gulp. Do I have a choice?*

He must have seen my face. "Plenty of treats in it for you, if you do it," he smiled.

*Treats, you say?*

We set off in Gapp's truck to the airfield. As we got closer and closer to the planes, Bill had to cover my ears again. It was real noisy. A plane whooshed over my head and another growled above me as it got ready to land.

"I'll tell the guys what's goin' on!" Gapp shouted above the noise. "And get the mechanics to finish off their engine work too."

He rushed off, while Bill explained to me again what he wanted me to do. When Gapp came back, he motioned for us to walk with

---

[41] Fighting on Luzon continued and casualties during the war were high. Over 8,000 Americans were killed in action, nearly 30,000 wounded and many missing in action, while the lives of over 170,000 Japanese were lost and over 7,000 declared missing in action.

him. Gapp and Bill's boots clacked as we walked across the airstrip, but thankfully it had gotten a whole heap quieter. I don't think I could have done anything while all that noise was going on. We walked along the edge of the airstrip until Gapp stopped and bent down.

"OK, the pipe runs sixty feet along there, and here's the phone wire." He smacked the palm of his hand against a wheel of wire. "Will Smoky hold it in her teeth?"

"Tell you what," Bill said, crouching down and inspecting the pipe, while I gave it a little sniff too. "If I fix the wire to her collar and tie a string leash around too, I can pull her back out if she gets stuck."

"You're the boss, Bill," Gapp said. "You too, Smoky. OK, I'll wait here with Smoky. Bill, if you run to the other end, give us the thumbs up and let's go for it."

*You mean, let* me *go for it!*

Bill fastened the wire and a length of string around my collar. Then I watched as he ran across to the other side of the airstrip. He bent down and put his thumb up. "OK!"

"Are you ready, Smoky?" Gapp grinned and patted my you-know-what.

*No need for that!*

I looked up at him. Then at the pipe. Then into the pipe. It looked like the open mouth of a scary creature just waiting to swallow me up. It was the darkest dark I'd ever seen. Much darker than when I wore the blindfold. I'm not exaggerating this time.

*I suppose this is going to mess my hair up too.*

Not for the first time when playing with Bill, I took a deep breath.
I crept into the pipe. My! I could barely fit inside and couldn't see a
thing. Not a thing! I set off as fast as I could, which wasn't very fast
at all as I kept having to clamber over mounds of earth. It smelled of

damp earth too.

*I'm back in the hole!*

My heart started to pound. I heard something behind me. A tree root! I scampered and scrabbled and crawled. Another mound of earth.

*How did it even get in here?*

I pushed my way through. I felt my collar pull back. I pushed on. I wanted to turn back, but couldn't even turn around.

*Must keep moving forward. Keep going. Think of Bill, think of Bill.*

I scampered on. More earth. Keep going.

*Where's Bill?*

I thought of Major.

*Run! Run!*

My collar pulled again. I started to pant.

*I can't do it!*

I thought of Major again.

*I have to do it! I have to! I'm wire walking! I'm wire walking! Bill! Bill!*

I carried on. Crawling now. What was that? I sniffed the air. I felt a slight breeze. "Come on, come on, Smoky. You can do it!" Bill's voice in my head.

A light in the distance. Another scent. Bill!

*I've done it. I've done it. He's there!*

I scrabbled and scampered. The light got bigger, the scent stronger. I heard Bill's voice for real.

"Smoky! Smoky! Here girl!"

Back leg. Front leg. Back leg. Front leg. I could see Bill's hand reaching in.

*Closer. Closer. Nearly there. Yesss!*

A lick of a hand, a hand under my belly and I was pulled out and up, the string and wire dangling down behind me.

"Lookee here!" Bill cried, gripping me tight. "I think I've got myself a bona fide war dog."

That night I could barely move for all the hugging and squeezing I'd gotten from all the GIs. Not to mention from the huge steak I was given as a reward.

*Yum! Divine!*

"And to think you don't even know how much you've helped the Pacific Campaign," Gapp grinned as he tickled me under my by now more than full tummy. "You've saved us so much time. Stopped our planes from being bombed out too. Well done, war dog, we're so proud of you!"[42]

---

[42] As a result of Smoky's obedience and trust in Bill's commands, the communication network was established, and she was credited with saving the lives of some 250 men and 40 planes that day.

Not another change of name!

I didn't mind, though. I was getting treat after treat after treat. To see Bill looking so happy after such a long time though was the biggest treat of all. As I watched Bill, I caught the scent of Petrilak. He came in with Kalt. They both looked real sad.

*Haven't they heard the news?*

Petrilak whispered something to Bill. Bill came over to me, lifted me up and squeezed me tight.

"There's been a disease in this camp the last few days and, well, Topper must've caught it. I'm real sorry, Smoky. But Topper's gone."

*Gone? What does he mean, gone? Where is he? Let me find him! Grrr...*

But Bill didn't set me down. He just held me instead. Long enough for me to realize that, just like so many GIs, Topper wouldn't be coming back.[43]

I felt the whirlwind swallowing me up and blowing me away. There I was being told I was a war dog but, at that moment, all I really wanted to be was a mummy dog.

---

[43] A sudden disease killed several dogs and many chickens in the area.

# 13 Harnessing

We had left Luzon in the Philippines and were in a place called Okinawa[44] when it happened. I was playing the running-through-the-legs-for-food game. It helped me to not think about Major. And Topper of course. A solemn voice boomed out and echoed in the room.

"Sshhh. It's President Truman," Gapp said quietly.

All the men stopped eating and fell silent. I had no clue where the voice was coming from.

"A short time ago, an American airplane dropped one bomb on Hiroshima and destroyed its usefulness to the enemy. That bomb had more power than 20,000 tons of TNT. The Japanese began their war from the air at Pearl Harbour. And they have been repaid many fold. It is an atomic bomb. It is a harnessing of the basic power of the universe. The force from which the sun draws its power has been loosed against those who brought war to the Far East...

"... We have spent more than two billion dollars on the greatest scientific gamble in history. And won."[45]

It felt as if every single man in the room drew in his biggest breath.

---

[44] The battle of Okinawa was the largest amphibious landing in the Pacific area during World War II. It resulted in the largest casualties with over 100,000 Japanese and 50,000 for the Allies. Over 80,000 local civilians lost their lives.
[45] August 6, 1945. August 15 was set as the date for World War II to officially end.

"We've done it," I heard Gapp say quietly.

*Done what?*

"They'll have to surrender now," Graham muttered.

I padded over to Bill's legs and jumped up onto his lap. I felt a drop of something hit me and looked up at him.

Tears were rolling down his face.

*****

It was real hot, as if the sun was melting around us. As hot as when Bill had set fire to the photo lab. Everything had all gotten real crazy for a while. I was so used to watching GIs move into, or set up, camps and call them home, but I couldn't understand why they were ripping tents down or smashing buildings into pieces.

Then there was Bill and the photo lab. I'd watched as he'd stepped inside it.

*What's he doing in there? Why am I not in there with him?*

When he came out, I saw thick, gray smoke coming out behind him. He picked me up and we stood back and watched as the gray smoke turned into real dark yellow flames. It felt so hot on my fur. I really didn't like it.

*I'm back on the ship! I'm back on the ship!*

I yipped until he stroked my head to calm me. Then he turned and walked away.

"Sorry, Smoky, I was a real long way away then. Was that too hot for you? Mighty strange to see all your work go up in smoke."

*Why is he doing it then?*

But now I was lying in the cool shadow of a truck with Bill. Graham and Barnard were sitting inside. Why didn't they sit in the shade with us? A crackling sound, music and voices kept coming from inside the truck.

*What's that?*

"Can't you get it tuned in?" I heard Graham snap at Barnard.

It was then I heard the low, distant rumbling. Oh no! I sprang up.

"It's OK, Smoky, it's OK," Bill said calmly. But he didn't look OK.

I started to bark and turn again, but Bill shouted, "Quiet, Smoky," real serious.

We watched as two small planes appeared in the distance. They got bigger as the rumbling got louder. I heard a strange crackling voice coming from the truck.

"Bataan I and Bataan II.[46] Come in. Identify yourselves."

Silence.

"Come on," I heard Graham cry from inside the truck. "Respond with the code or we'll knock you clean out of the air."

More silence.

I looked at Bill, then up at the planes, then back at Bill again.

---

[46] The codes the Japanese pilots were required to give as they brought in their envoys to sign the peace treaty.

*Where is he looking?*

Another crackling sound came from inside the truck, and then, an even stranger crackling voice.

"Bataan I and Bataan II. We can hear you."

Bill and the others all let out the biggest breath.

"They've surrendered. It really is a peace envoy." Bill's face broke into a huge smile and he looked right at me. Then he lay down on the ground, his arms outstretched above his head, the biggest smile I'd ever seen across his face. Even bigger than when I'd played the run-through-the pipe game.

My head started to spin a little, at the way Bill was lying all stretched out, a sense of the familiar… I skipped over to Bill and licked his face. He reached out and stroked my back. "It's over, Smoky. We can go home."

*Oh no! Not another home!*

*****

I was running in and out of the legs of Bill, Petrilak, Barnard and Graham. It was so much better now that Bill was around for more fun and, even though a lot of men were leaving and not coming back, even if the camp was getting smaller and more broken, everyone was much happier.

"Hey, guys, you wanna see somethin'?" Bill asked the others.

"Sure," they replied.

"Right, Smoky. Heel," Bill commanded, and I trotted right over to him. He'd got those shapes and spread them out on the ground.

*Oh, here we go!*

"What's your name, Smoky? What's your name?"

*He's gone crazy again! Surely he knows my name by now?*

But I knew what he wanted me to do. It was the shape game of course. The one I'd found real hard for such a long time. After days and days and days, though, after 'S' and 'S' and 'S' and after Bill pointing and pointing at one shape, I realized it looked just like that scary, curled-up tree root. After more days and days and Bill pointing and saying 'M' and 'M', the shape he pointed at started to look like the tables the GIs sat and ate at. And it took me even more days to see the 'O' shape looked like Bill's helmet. But, no matter how much I looked at the two other shapes, I just couldn't tell them apart, so I'd always get the game wrong.

But! But! Now, I was sure I'd figured it out. The 'K' shape looked like one of my stepladders and the 'Y' was the same shape as... as Bill when he was on the ground all happy and smiling with his arms outstretched.

*That's it! Yesss! I can read!*

"Tell us your name, Smoky," Bill smiled.

"It's Smoky," I barked, but Bill just laughed.

"Go on," he continued. "Find 'S'."

I looked at the shapes. The helmet, the table, the curly tree root.

*There it is!*

I ran over to the curly tree root shape.

"Well done, Smoky!" Bill bent down and gave me a treat. "And where's 'M'? Find 'M'."

Easy! I ran to the shape that looked like a table. Petrilak, Barnard and Graham looked on, wide eyed.

"And now 'O', Smoky. Find 'O'," Bill said, after I'd swallowed another treat.

I looked at all the shapes again. That one looks like Bill's helmet. And that one looks like a stepladder. Or is it that one? Never mind.

I scampered over to the shape of Bill's helmet and pounced on it. I got another treat and a huge cheer from the others.

"Now Smoky. Where's 'K'?"

I stared at the two remaining shapes.

*That one's the stepladder. That one! The other looks like Bill stretched out. So which one does he want me to run to again? The stepladder or Bill stretched out? Stepladder or Bill? Stepladder or Bill? I can't remember what comes next!*

I looked and looked at them both. Days and days passed.

*Ahhh well. Here we go…*

I dived onto Bill.

His face dropped a little and he gave a little shrug.

"Shucks. Guess you can't win 'em all!"

## 14 Snapping

Now the whirlwind blows me from Okinawa to Korea. I feel like I'm jumping around again. It's taking me everywhere, even places I don't wanna be. Like when we were waiting and waiting to leave and it whooshed around inside me. It wasn't warm, not like this one, but burned. A nasty burn from my head, down to my tail. And I'm real certain Pepper felt it as well. Pepper was my friend, she belonged to Zeitlin. She was a real puppy.

*Why does Zeitlin get to keep his puppy when I don't get to keep mine?*

Bill must have known the whirlwind was inside me too.

"I'm takin' you to the War Dog Platoon," he said. "See if we can find you a vet."

Turns out he took me to a hospital for dogs, but I couldn't smell the fresh scent, the one that made my head spin. The burning whirlwind saw to that. But it didn't stop the smell of sickly dogs, or the sound of angry dogs. I heard the one guarding the entrance. He was a four-legged Downey. Worse. Bill told me he was a Shepherd. I just thought he was scary until I saw the lost look in his eyes.

*Maybe he has a whirlwind right inside him too?*

"So, it looks to me like a nasal infection," the medic said to Bill when it was finally our turn.

"Phew," Bill replied. "I was worried it might be scrub typhus."

115

"No. She'll be OK. But I'm afraid I'm all out of medicine. Try feedin' her fresh milk and eggs."

"Well, there ain't much chance of findin' you somethin' fresh," Bill said when we got back, my head still spinning. "But I've mixed up some powdered egg and dehydrated milk in water for you. Here, try some of this… "

I gulped it down. Bleurgh! It sure didn't taste like the milk we'd had in Brisbane, but I got used to it. And it did help with the burning. I don't think Pepper ever got to try it though. The whirlwind must have got to her. Just like how it got to my Topper. And just like the real huge whirlwind we found ourselves slap bang in the middle of right as we had been about to leave Okinawa.[47] One that blew all our tents away and soaked us all, soaked us all through before we moved onward to Kimpo in Korea.

"We're getting closer to home," Bill said.

More waiting and wondering.

*But where is home if not here?*

While we were waiting to move on to heaven knows where, Bill made a bag for me.

"Right, Smoky, when it's our turn to leave, you're gonna have to sit tight in this bag while I smuggle you on board. I've heard they throw dogs overboard if they find them and we sure ain't havin' anythin' happenin' to you. Not now. Not with all we've been through."

I didn't know what sounded worse. Having to get on a ship again

---

[47] A typhoon hit with winds up to 150 miles per hour, resulting in ships being lost, planes damaged, many deaths and injuries, as well as damage to military installations and housing.

or being thrown —splosh! — overboard if I got caught.

We played a game where I jumped in the bag, crouched down and had to keep quiet for a real long time. We played it and played it.

"You sure that's gonna work, Wynne?" Piwarski[48] asked Bill as he watched us.

"It will if I struggle on board with all our bags," Bill grinned. "And you sneak on carrying a lighter load 'cause you're wounded."

Piwarski's eyes widened and he let out a short laugh.

Then the truck arrived to take us to Incheon and I got to play the game for real.

"This is it, Smoky," Bill said softly as we sat in the back, squashed up against lots of other men. It was real packed and I was scared, but the smell of all those men together was a real comfort. Something else I'd gotten used to.

"You've really gotta be still and quiet now. If they catch you when we get to the ship, we'll both be in a whole heap of trouble."[49]

Bill must have felt me tremble and heard me whimper at the thought of being back on a ship again, because he put his mouth close to the zip of the bag and whispered, "You'll be safe, Smoky. The war's over."

*Has it gone? How does Bill know?*

I don't remember much about getting on board. I felt Bill handing me over to Piwarski and I snuggled right down in that bag. I heard lots of noises and shouting, but I didn't dare stick my head out. And

---

[48] Ed Piwarski.
[49] Army regulations stated no animals were permitted to travel on board back to the US.

117

it worked! We made it on board. Bill found a bed for us right in the corner of the ship. I saw his face peering down at me as he opened the bag.

"We did it, Smoky," he grinned. "We're on board the USS General W. H. Gordon. Should be plain sailing from now on."

I was real scared for the first few days. I was waiting to get caught, waiting for the war to come back, to hear the whistling sound again. The fear must have made Bill ill too. He turned light yellow and had to eat dark yellow fruit called oranges, so Piwarski had to look after me for a while.

"That's the trouble with Wynne," Piwarski whispered to me as he took me on a secret walk late one night. "No sea legs. Not like you."

*Sea legs? My scampering legs are fine and dandy. Yes sirree.*

I didn't mind being with Piwarski while Bill was poorly. Me and Bill hadn't gone down together. Despite the whirlwinds and the missions, we were still together. Had the war really gone? I began to feel less scared and more brave.

But one day, a crackling voice echoed around the ship. "Will all men with dogs or monkeys on board report to the ship's office immediately."

*Gulp!*

I was braver, but not completely brave. Bill's face had just gotten back to being light gray when he suddenly looked ill again.

"I'd best go see what's up," and he left me, trembling, with Piwarski.

Bill came back, smiling.

"We've been reprieved, Smoky! Dogs can stay. But the monkeys have to go."

Even though I knew that Colonel Turbo was one, and he hadn't exactly been friendly to me, I didn't like to think about how they got those monkeys off the ship…

We'd been on board for ten days before I heard the squawking coming from outside. I knew it was that long because Bill was counting them down. "Only four days to go, Smoky… Only two days… Not long now… "

We dashed out on deck to find out what all the noise was about. I sat in Bill's arms and saw huge, light gray birds flying overhead. Then I looked down to see where all the other noise was coming from. A small boat, rammed full with men and women, sailed toward us. They were cheering and singing and holding up signs.

"Look at what they've done for us!" Bill cried. "They're saying 'Well Done! Welcome Home!'"

The signs didn't say that to me. I could just about make out some tables and Bill's helmet on them.

The singing boat sailed alongside us the rest of the way, but was nothing compared to the crowds of people waiting for us when the ship docked. We were given a heck of a welcome when we finally stepped off. Yes sirree. Everyone wanted to hold me, while others clicked and snapped away. They all had cameras, just like Bill did.

We slept in a comfy bed in a building, and me and Bill were given lots more pictures, like those on my blanket, which had had more things sewn on it.[50] Best of all though was the food. Mmm. Yum!

---

[50] Bill and his colleagues were awarded several ribbons and awards including the Victory Medal, Good Conduct Medal, Asiatic Pacific Campaign Ribbon and the Philippine Liberation Ribbon. 'Smoky Champion Yank Mascot SWPA 1944' was added to Smoky's blanket by a local lady in the Philippines.

Fresh, fresh milk and the juiciest meat ever called T-bone steak. We even both had a haircut as well. I didn't mind this time though. Bill must've told them what I wanted because, when the man had finished cutting and brushing and blowing, it was as if all the mud and the rain and especially the war, were finally, finally behind me. Not to mention feeling like the most divine girl for the first time in a long time!

After that, we had to get something called a train. Trucks, ships, planes, trains, I never knew there were so many ways to move around. Before I met Bill, all I could do was run and jump. Now, not only was I dancing, walking on wires and balancing on oil drums, but I'd been on water, flown higher than I could ever jump and moved much, much faster than I could run. I was sad when Duke ran off somewhere after we got off the boat. Bill said it was a real shame after all Duke had been through in the war and all that his friend, Shorty Randall, did to try and get him safely back home.

And then we arrived home. Bill's real home, he said it was. And my new home. My! I'd never seen people so happy and unhappy at the same time! Laughing and crying, talking and singing.

Bill introduced me to someone called Mom and another nice lady called Margie. They both looked so clean and smelled real good. I didn't really know who Mom was, but she sure hugged and hugged Bill when we arrived at her house. Margie too, before she stopped hugging him and pointed at me.

"What about Toby and Lucky?" Margie said to Bill. "D'you think they'll take to him?"

"Her," Bill answered softly but firmly. "And I dunno. But we'll soon see."

Toby and Lucky lived with Mom in her huge, comfy home. Toby was a dog.

"Who's this? Who's this? Who's this?" Toby came bounding

over to me.

"Hey, stop whining, Toby," Bill laughed as Toby jumped around us both. "This here's Smoky."

"Smoky, yes? Smoky." Toby barked and jumped up at Bill. "Just let me finish saying hello to Bill. It's been days and days and days…"

I waited for Toby to stop jumping. It was then I saw Lucky. He was a dark, dark gray cat. He eyeballed me slowly from the doorway and hissed.

*Uh-oh. Think I'd better steer clear of Lucky for now. And what sort of silly name is Lucky, anyway?*

But it sure was nice to be with Bill and all these other people. Back in the jungle, all the men used to look the same and smell the same. Here though, in this new home, everybody looked and smelled different, all fresh, new and clean. Smiling too; no one seemed lost. There was plenty of food for me to eat, I had a new friend in Toby, and lots of other men and women wanted to meet me. It was real fun.

Me and Bill went somewhere called the Cleveland Press. Bill tried to explain it to me, but none of it made any sense. All I knew was that a lady called a reporter asked Bill a whole heap of questions about me.[51] She wanted to know how Bill found me and what tricks I could do. My, she sure wanted to know everything about me.

"D'you want a ride on your scooter?" Bill asked me when we were with Eleanor, the reporter.

*You bet I do!*

---

[51] Maxwell Riddle, one of the world's leading authorities on dogs, originally phoned Bill, but was in hospital at the time of the interview so Eleanor Prech took his place. Riddle has judged dog shows worldwide and is the author of numerous books about dogs.

Riding on the scooter was another game that Bill played with me while we were waiting and waiting to leave Okinawa, before the long, long journey here.

It had three wheels and I had to sit on the little seat, put my front paws on the bar in front of me and move my back legs up and down. The scooter went around and around in a circle. Then I'd yip while everyone stood around, laughing and clapping.

"That's quite a show dog you got there, Bill,"

*Show dog? I thought I was a war dog?*

Eleanor beamed at us. "Mind if we take some more pictures?"

I rode around while lots of other reporters came in and someone arrived and took lots of pictures of me doing everything Bill told me to do. The snapping and snapping of cameras reminded me of being back in Bill's helmet.

"Look here, you two," Mom said to us the next day.

*Uh-oh! More reading.*

Bill grabbed the large magazine.

"General Yamashita's been sentenced to death," he muttered.

"Not that. There."

Bill read out loud, "'Tiny Dog Home From The War.' Wow, Smoky. A double-page spread. Look."

I didn't want to look, so I just sniffed it. It still just looked like lots of squiggles. What did any of that have to do with me?

After that, we had to go somewhere called a radio studio. It was

122

like being back in the photo lab, all dark and hot. A man called Bob Neal[52] asked Bill lots of questions about me again. I knew all there was to know about me so, while Bill answered them, I had a nice snooze on his lap.

"So, what's next for you two?" I heard Bob ask as Bill gently shook me awake.

What's next was meeting someone called Captain Arthur Roth.[53] He was from the Police Department and he looked a little like my GI friends except his uniform was dark, dark gray and his helmet was flat. Captain Roth had a huge snarling dog with him called Silver King.[54] As Bill and Captain Roth talked, I sniffed Silver King out.

"I hear you've been in the war," Silver King growled as he towered above me. "Bet you've seen some things."

"Yes. I didn't see the war though," I answered, trying not to sound scared. "I just felt it."

"I heard different. I heard they call you a war dog." And I saw in Silver King's eyes the same look Bill got whenever I'd done something real good, like pulling the wire through the dark tunnel.

Silver King told me he used to be a police dog. He used to chase men, jump up at them and wrestle them to the floor. "That's how I lost a front tooth," Silver King snarled, but it was a friendly snarl.

Captain Roth was looking down at us. "So, how d'ya fancy it?" Me and Silver King both looked up at Bill and Roth.

"A week's tour around Cleveland visiting some needy kids? They'd sure love to see you dogs showing off. Besides, at Christmas

---

[52] Radio broadcaster who had a regular "Sport Spotlight" slot.
[53] He was working with juveniles at the time, often in neighbourhoods with issues.
[54] A German Shepherd who traveled the country with his owner to give traffic safety demonstrations.

time, they need all the company they can get."

That word again!

I barked and yipped and barked.

"Well, it sure seems like your Smoky wants to do it," Roth laughed. "Better get you booked in before you both become real famous."

## 15 Spinning

I could just about make out the muffled voice. "Ladies and gentlemen, boys and girls. Please put your hands together for Bill Wynne and his dog, Corporal Smoky!"

I bristled at the sound of the crowd, of people clapping their hands together and at the jolt as Bill lifted me up and carried me out onto the stage. I knew what was coming, what to expect. I'd performed this hundreds of times now.[55] If I really pricked my ears up, I could hear Bill telling the audience about the foxhole, about him buying me for two pounds Australian, about all the games and training, which I loved, and the ships and the howling, which I didn't.

When Bill had finished talking, he'd open the zipper and up I'd pop out of the bag. The crowds would gasp before clapping again, although not as loud as when I got to play all my favourite games on stage with Bill. I would dance with him to music, ride on my scooter or jump on top of the barrel. Sometimes I'd play my own games with Bill too, like stand right in the middle of the tightrope wires pretending I was scared, or run around hurdles instead of over them. Well, I did like to keep Bill on his toes too!

The more I saw people watching and enjoying us perform, the more I played and showed off. How I loved being the center of attention! But it wasn't always lots and lots of happy people we performed to. No sirree. I'd still go into hospitals sometimes — my

---

[55] Bill and Smoky performed at many Christmas shows in December 1945 for local companies and fraternal organizations, often with band accompaniment. "Pretty Baby" was a favorite as Smoky walked in and out of Bill's legs, or the "Funeral March" when she played dead.

nose sniffing the air of course — and visit the ones who lived there.

After the war, I didn't know why some men and women smiled and seemed real happy, while others still seemed so sad and lost. Especially the ones in the hospitals. In one called Crile Hospital,[56] the nurses sat me on the lap of a man sitting in a chair on wheels. He sure looked like one of the sad ones. A nurse lifted his hand and placed it on my back. After a while, I felt his fingers start to move against my fur, and I looked up to see his face had changed. He smiled and started to rock me back and forth, then I glanced over at the nurses. They were all doing the confusing laughing-crying I'd seen Mom and Margie do when Bill and I had arrived home. Some of them were using small blankets to dab at their faces.

"Jefferson's been catatonic ever since he was transferred here," I heard one of the nurses saying to Bill. "He hasn't responded to any stimulus for two years. This is the first time we've ever seen him like this."

It was real strange to see people smiling when I played around on stage and others smiling when all I did was cuddle up to them. It must be my lovely long hair!

Whoosh...

"Where's Smoky? Where is she?" I heard Bill bound in and ask Mom and Margie excitedly. I shot out from my hidey place and raced downstairs to find him.

"Guess what, Smoky? We've been invited to join the circus!"[57]

*A whattus?*

---

[56] A local army hospital.
[57] Al Sirat Grotto Circus performed annually at the Public Hall in Cleveland. Bill and Smoky received a contract for eight days of performances in February 1946.

I soon got to find out what a circus was. I never knew there were so many other creatures in the world! Huge dark gray ones, tiny light gray ones and everything in between. And the stench! My, I really wasn't sure if I wanted to be friends with any of them, not the big scary ones who looked like they would crush li'l ole me in a heartbeat, and not the real smelly ones, that's for certain. It sure was noisy too when they were all calling out to each other. Oh, of course I had no idea what any of them were saying!

But they weren't half as noisy as when I heard the BOOM! BOOM! BOOM! and shrank right back. Bill told me it was just the sound of cannons firing and it wouldn't do me any harm but, still, I'd just look for the nearest hole to dive into whenever I heard the dreadful, dreadful sound.

The circus tent was big, much, much bigger than the ones we'd slept in or even the ones we'd eaten in. The circus show started, the tent was packed out with lots and lots of people wanting to watch but, by the end, there were only a few left. The children had fallen asleep and the adults were looking real tired. I knew how they felt, I had to wait and wait to go into the ring and play around with Bill. Then, after me, others would go into the ring and show off their tricks and then some real scary looking people Bill said were called clowns joined in. That circus show sure did last a real long time. I didn't know why it didn't just end after I'd performed!

The whirlwind whooshes me forward again, to the time when Bill took me to see a woman called Goldie.[58]

"I've read about you in the papers," Goldie beamed when she opened her door to us. "So I just had to invite you guys over and show you my little brood." Goldie owned sixteen dogs in all. Bill counted them. They all looked and smelled just like me. I'd never met a dog that looked just like me before, never mind sixteen of them. That was real fun. Yes sirree. They looked so pretty too with their

---

[58] Goldie Stone, a Yorkie breeder from Columbus, Ohio.

long hair and bows and ribbons. And my! The noise we made as we all said hello!

"I've been breeding them ever since Charlie and I quit performing," Goldie explained to Bill as he held me in his arms.[59] I could see the me-dogs in the other room. Why wouldn't Goldie and Bill let me play with them?

*Put me down! Let me play! Grrrr. Why can't I play with them?*[60]

"I can see that Smoky's a typy dog,"[61] Goldie said as she examined me all over. "How're you finding all the fame?" She asked with a smile.

"She's lovin' it," Bill answered, rubbing my head.

*Fame? What's that? Is it like war again? Something to feel but not see?*

"Much more than when we were out fightin'," Bill continued. "I'm tryin' to get it all down on paper, me and Smoky have sure lived an interestin' few years, but I'm not sure there's much interest in the war now. Seems that folks jus' wanna forget about it and get on with life."

"Mebbe Smoky here's getting it all down," Goldie smiled again.

The whirlwind! It's coming again. I can feel the rushing inside of me pushing me somewhere else. It's hurting now too. Deep in my tummy...

---

[59] Goldie and her husband had featured at various circuses, calling themselves Stone and Stone, with speciality acts of tightrope walking and a balancing act.
[60] The Stones refused entry to their house for dogs without a quarantine. Smoky became the sole exception, though she was not allowed to play with the other dogs.
[61] A good specimen of the breed.

I am in the Traveling Zoo.[62] Every time we stop, we meet people who want to ask Bill lots of questions about me and take pictures of me.

"These kids don't get opportunities like this," Bill explained to me. "And they sure haven't met anyone like you before. You know some of these kids have come over a dozen times just to see you. You're a star, Smoky."

We visited playgrounds when the days were long and hot and lots of children would come to see us. I would ride my bike, dance to music or even 'say my prayers,' a new trick that Bill had taught me.

"Say your prayers, Smoky," Bill would command and I'd jump onto someone's lap, rest on my back legs and hold my two front paws together. They loved that!

In between times, I'd listen and try to understand what all the other creatures in the zoo were saying, or try to remember what they were all called.

"That's a raccoon," Bill would point to something that was much bigger than me, with lovely light gray and dark gray fur. "And that's an armadillo," and he'd point to a creature that sure didn't look anything like me.

*Where's all its fur gone?*

We went to a dog shelter too, a sad place where dogs went when they had no place to call a home of their own. It made me realize how lucky I was to find Bill. I met all sorts of big dogs and small dogs and immediately recognized the lost look in their sad eyes. As I posed for yet another photo in Bill's arms he told me, "This is for the *Chicago*

---

[62] A show of zoo animals, performing four times a day, five days each week. Many spectators had never seen animals before, with over 1,000 people in the audience on occasions, drawing over 100,000 people in only ten weeks.

*Tribune.* The phone's really gonna go off the hook after this."

And he was right. I wasn't sure what off the hook meant, but the phone did ring a crazy lot.[63] It always tickled me when Bill held it up to his mouth and talked, as if he was speaking to someone else. At first, I thought he was talking to me, but I got used to it.

"OK, OK," Bill said into it one day, all serious. "And we'll be doing what again?" Bill stood there, silent, still holding the strange phone thing up to his ear. He started to smile. It got wider and wider.

"I gotcha. And when d'you want us to be there?"

He was beaming even more when he put the phone down.

"What is it? What is it?" Margie asked, wide eyed.

"We're going to Hollywood!" he cried, so loud it made me jump.

"Oh, wow, Bill, that's wonderful news." But then her face dropped a little. "But what about our wedding?"[64]

"Oh, don't worry," Bill said finally, flopping into a chair. I jumped up onto his lap.

"We don't need to be there till afterwards. Whaddya say we go as part of our honeymoon?"

"I was hoping for some sunshine," said Margie standing over him. "Not you having to work. Besides, how are we going to get there?"

How we got there was in a beautiful, light, light gray car called a Packard Super 8. I only knew that, of course, because Bill told me as

---

[63] Bill and Smoky performed at numerous different venues and were interviewed time and again.

[64] The date was set for September 28, 1946.

he was inspecting it.

"Look at the nickel-plated radiator, Smoky. And the bumpers! Ain't she a beaut'?"

I tried to be as excited about it as Bill was. But to me it just looked like one of the trucks back in the jungle. Oh sure, it was much cleaner, smelled divine inside and was very smooth and comfy to ride in when we finally did set off, but it was a truck just the same.

"Hollywood, here we come!" yelled Bill out of the window as we drove and drove.

"Sshh, be quiet Bill," said Margie, leaning right down in her seat at the front.

I was in the back, my head could just about make it out of the window. I could feel my ears and hair streaming behind me again, just like when I was on the ship. Wheee!

The sky was as blue as it had been when I was on the ship too. Gradually though it changed from dark blue to dark gray. And then the rain and thunder started.

I yipped and yipped as the rain dripped onto my head. Margie turned around to close my window.

"Bill, the roof's leaking! The roof!"

"Can't look now, Margie!" he cried. "I can barely see where I'm going."

It was so dark outside. I watched the rain on the windows as it lashed down all around. I felt it drip, drip, drip onto my head.

*Where's my blanket?*

I heard a screech. "Woah!" Bill cried and we started to spin. Around and around we went. My tummy flew outside of me.

*What's happening?*

A crunch and we came to a sudden stop. Bill and Margie looked at each other. They were both pale and shaking.

"You all right?" Bill asked Margie. "That was some skid."

"I think so. You?"

Bill nodded. "And how about you, Smoky?" he said, turning around.

I was OK. I had gotten used to being without my tummy from time to time. I gave him a little yip, but I didn't wag my tail. I tried to look out of the window again.

*Well, if this is Hollywood. I don't think much of it...*

# 16 Brooding

It's getting darker now. Real dark. I can hear Bill's voice and, if I roll my head to the side, I can just about make out his concerned face peering through the darkness. But it feels as if I'm slipping down a hole and he's moving further away. The light gets smaller, Bill's voice gets fainter, the darkness wraps around me, but I am warm, comfortable…

A fanfare jolts me awake. Out of the darkness, a huge, huge rectangle of light almost blinds me. I can hear people moving around in their plush seats next to me, but I can't see all of them. The seats are all facing the rectangle of light. It turns into the biggest dog I've ever seen. It stares down and towers above us all, but I'm not scared. It's a dog I recognize. It's Elmer, one of the dogs that Bill was working with.[65] Well, Bill said it was work, but it all looked just like playing to me. He'd told me a lot about working with Elmer.

"I've been training a real wild one today. He even had the brass neck to bite Jimmy Stewart on set,"[66] Bill said when he got back and tickled me hello after a long day without him. He'd just walked in through the door of the Hollywood apartment we were staying in. There was so much room in that apartment for me to run around and explore. I could play hide and seek for days and days and Bill would have no idea where to find me unless I yipped and yipped and gave the game away.

"I've really got my work cut out getting him ready for the big screen. Why can't they all be as clever as you, Smoky?"

---

[65] Bill was training Elmer for a role in one of the *Blondie* movies.
[66] Jimmy Stewart was working on the film *Magic Town* at the time.

133

At first I didn't like being in the apartment with Margie, waiting for Bill to come back. I'd smell other dogs on him when he returned and I didn't like it. No sirree.

*Why isn't he spending time with* me?

But I think Bill sensed I wasn't happy about it because, every so often, he used to take me to where he worked. I watched him playing around with other dogs, shake his head, then play the exact same game with them again. But still they didn't get it right.

*Why don't they just do as he asks? It's such an easy way to get lovely treats.*

After I'd seen Bill playing at work with these other dogs, I felt much happier. I mean, Bill couldn't like the dogs more than me — I was clearly better at playing than them. Most of the games they were playing I could have done with my blindfold on and, besides, not one of them had hair as long and as pretty as mine!

I didn't know why Bill would play games with me and sometimes take pictures of me, but I never saw him take pictures of the other dogs he played with. I wondered if it was because I was special to Bill, but then I saw the dogs he'd played with on giant pictures in a big, dark room. And the giant pictures were moving!

*So if I'm special, why can't I get to be in a giant picture that moves too?*

I don't think Margie understood it all either. She and Bill would talk a lot in the apartment. I think Margie wanted to move back to Cleveland, but Bill was happy being in Hollywood.

"I'm not quite sure if this new climate agrees with me, Bill. There must be something in the air. I've been feeling sickly for weeks."

"And I'm sorry to leave you on your lonesome so much. I never knew the hours at the studio would be so long. But we'll work something out."

"Well, I sure hope we will, Bill. We've only been married three months and I'm starting to feel like some kind of... Hollywood widow while you train dogs for the movies," Margie replied with a small smile.

Then they'd do that thing where their mouths would touch and make a funny noise. There wasn't even any room for me to squeeze in between them.

After a lot more talking, Margie decided to go back to Cleveland and so me and Bill moved into a cabin. It was much smaller than the apartment and it sure wasn't as nice.

"Never mind, Smoky," Bill said, sniffing and looking around. "If you can survive jungles, tents and tropical storms, then this'll be a walk in the park for you."

Walk in the park? I headed straight for the cabin door when Bill said that.

There was no walk in the park though, not on that day at least. Instead, I'd go to work with Bill, watch him with the other dogs and then we'd return to the small, stuffy cabin when it got real dark. Bill was making me a new collar when the phone thing made the loud noise that always made me bark.

Bill ran over to it and picked it up.

"Hello. Hi, honey, how's Cleveland... and how are you? You've got some what? I can't hear you. You're what? Really? Oh, wow, that sure is amazin'!" And I saw a smile on his face bigger than when I learnt to walk on wires, as big as when the war was over.

After Bill had stopped speaking into the phone thing, he put it down and wiped his eyes. He picked me up, hugged me and told me Margie was pregnant. I had no clue what he meant by that. No clue at all.

Whoosh!

And now it was getting light. Hotter too. I was on stage again. "Your second home," Bill said once. But by that time I'd been on so many stages and in front of so many audiences that surely it must have been my... whatever-a-lot-more-than-second-is home. Besides, it didn't feel like home. Home meant being with Bill, not always warm and safe — not when we were in the jungle anyway — but knowing there was at least someone around to look after me.

Being on stage meant showing off in front of lots of people, maybe even getting away with things that I couldn't have gotten away with at home; like the time I'd couldn't stop drinking and drinking water because it was so darn hot and ended up letting it go on stage. Everyone laughed when I did that. Even Bill, but I'm real sure he wouldn't have laughed if I'd done that at home.

The stage was in Ohio. We were going to be in a show with lots of other creatures. "Say 'hi' to Ohio when we get there!" Bill grinned We'd got there on a huge bus, with all the creatures who'd be playing their own games on stage travelling in cages at the back. Bill pointed them out to me as we trooped on board.

"Look at the fantastic mane on that lion, Smoky. And there's a bear. Look, some eagles. There's Charlie the Pathe rooster and Gallant Bass the movie star horse. You'll be sharing a stage with all those Smoky. How d'you feel about *that?*"

I felt small. All the other creatures were so, so huge compared to me. Even Charlie the cock-a-doodle-do-ing rooster and scary looking eagles could have picked me up and flown off with me if they got half a chance. I really didn't like the look of those. No sirree.

As we traveled on the bus, there was a great squawking coming from the back. Bill tucked me under his arm and went to take a look. It was one of the eagles, rocking back and forth. It kept falling off its perch in the cage. For some reason, it reminded me of the poor men we'd visited in the hospitals.

Bill opened the cage to pick the bird up but, as he did so, the eagle flapped its huge wings and knocked Bill right over.

"Ouch!" Bill cried. "My shoulder."

So, even though I did manage to bark 'hi' to Ohio when we arrived there, because of Bill's sore shoulder it was one of the few times that I actually watched a show instead of performing in it. It was still real fun watching the horse, lion and all the others playing, but not as much fun as me being in it of course. I felt sorry for the audience too. They sure didn't know what they were missing!

And I didn't know what I was missing either… Well, I suppose I did. How could I ever forget…?

By the time Bill and Margie came back from the hospital with their brand new puppy person, I'd started to feel real strange. Their puppy person was a girl, like me, only a bit bigger and with far less hair. I liked her, but I just felt stranger and stranger, until the day I had another puppy of my own. I guess I'd been feeling different, somehow, since Bill had taken me to meet Goldie and her sixteen me-dogs. Bill had gotten himself one he called Terry and I'd played a real fun, quick game with him. So Bill and Margie had their puppy person and I had a puppy of my own. And my Bobby sure was a sweetie!

*I really hope a whirlwind doesn't come for Bobby like one did for Topper.*

Bill and Margie called their puppy person Joanne Marie and they looked after her, while I looked after Bobby, but Bobby didn't cry half as much as Joanne Marie.

137

Our performances didn't stop, though. When Bill wasn't looking after Joanne Marie and I wasn't licking and cleaning my little bundle, we'd go out to nightclubs and perform.

I still enjoyed running along the wire with the blindfold, I loved balancing on the barrel too, but what I loved most of all was meeting people afterwards. They would hug and stroke me, take pictures just like Bill used to and ask him lots of questions about me. How I wished I could tell them about being hot in the jungle, being cold in the planes, being scared on the ships and being so happy when I was playing with Bill and his friends!

Once a week, we went to a hot television studio, where Bill said lots and lots of people could see me, but I couldn't see them. He was real excited when he told me we were going to be on *Polka Review*, one of the first shows ever shown on television in Cleveland.

"Hey, Smoky, we've got another one," Bill shouted to me soon after it, when he had spoken to the phone again. "They've asked us to do *Castles In The Air,* once a week for thirteen weeks!"

*What* is *he talking about?*

"Come on, Smoky, we're on soon." I heard Bill's voice. My nose twitched as I smelled his scent.

*Is that Bill? Why's he wearing that silly hair and what happened to his nose?*[67]

"What d'you think of my costume, Smoky?" he asked. "Like a tramp."

No, I didn't like it! His trousers were torn and he had funny bags over his shoes for a start.

---

[67] Bill donned a wig and false nose, wore crazy clothes and adopted a squeaky voice for this act.

"Who are you?" a lady asked as we went on.

*I wish I knew.*

"Mr. Pokie and my dog, Smoky."

*Ah, that's me. But why's Bill changed his name now? And why's he got a silly voice?*

He let me walk my tightrope that day.

*Another treat. Yum.*

It was hot under all the lights, but the men with their big cameras smiled a lot and I knew I'd made them happy.

We went back every week and each time I did another trick.

"Forty-two shows, Smoky," Bill said, a long time later. "Forty-two! And without repeating a single trick! What a star you are." He gave me an extra treat every time I spelled my name correctly too. I'd surprised him with my reading in Korea one day, when he wasn't pushing me to try the spelling trick. Sometimes I liked to let him see I could be the boss.

The day our new friend, Rudd,[68] was watching, Bill gave me a lot more treats for that trick too. Bill said he was proud of me when I did something that even Rudd thought was real, real clever. I don't know what he meant but, if it involved lots of treats, I would do it again and again.

Whoosh!

---

[68] Rudd Weatherwax, who trained many dogs, including Pal who played the infamous Lassie in numerous films.

"You've been featured in a magazine again, Smoky," Bill said to me excitedly. Another magazine. Another sniff.

*I don't know why he's so excited by magazines and newspapers, we've done hundreds.*

And I didn't know why I wasn't excited any more. Not that I was ever excited by the funny squiggles, but it made Bill happy, so I was happy too. But now things had changed.

Me, Bill, Margie, Joanne Marie and Bobby had been to see Helen, a lady who looked a bit like Margie,[69] but only me, Bill, Margie and Joanne Marie came back. I don't know why they forgot to bring Bobby back. I yapped and yapped on the way home, trying to tell Bill that we'd forgotten Bobby, but he didn't seem to understand me. They wouldn't forget Joanne Marie, would they?

"It's *American Magazine*," Bill continued. "And listen to this, Smoky. They've named you as 'One of The Most Useful Dogs in America.'"

I knew what useful meant. But did that mean it was another name for me to remember? And how useful was I really if I couldn't make Bill understand that I wanted Bobby back?

---

[69] Margie's sister.

# 17 Closing

I didn't ever see Bobby again.[70] He wasn't there the next time we went to visit Helen. I hunted and hunted and sniffed and sniffed, but I couldn't even smell him, much less find him. But now I see him! He's with Topper. I try to run toward them both...

"Smoky! Smoky! Visitor for you."

Where am I? Am I in Cleveland, in Bill and Margie's home, or am I in a hot television studio? Am I on *Castles In The Air* again?

No, I am here. With Bill. I am warm. I am comfortable. I am cushioned by darkness. I think back to the searing hot lights of the television studios, of Bill trying to explain to me what television was and how he thought it would never catch on. I think of all Bill and Margie's other puppy people that came along and, of course, I think of Topper and Bobby once more.

I think of the miles of driving around that me and Bill did to get to our performances, the hundreds and hundreds of people we met, the days and days and days we spent in Hollywood and under the hot, bright lights of television studios.

"Smoky! Hey, girl!"

I try to turn my head toward the voice, but it feels so, so heavy. I can just about make out two pairs of legs walking toward me. One is Bill's. The other legs are unfamiliar... but the scent isn't. It's the

---

[70] Smoky's pup became ill after eating something when playing outside and sadly died.

hospital smell! If I felt better, I'd be jumping up and down and barking without knowing why. Who is this visitor?

"Smoky," says Bill, crouching down next to me. I try to lick his hand. "This is Grace. She wanted to see you."

I hear Grace gasp. "My gosh. I thought I recognized her from the newspapers, but yes, it's her! Christmas! Oh, Christmas! I thought I'd never see you again!"[71]

I twitch at the sound of that word again and try to turn my head once more, but it hurts so much in my tummy. It hurts everywhere. I hear Grace's voice again.

"I was working in a hospital in Dobudura. She was just a puppy. The most gorgeous little thing. We were both in the ward. I was tending to a patient but, when I turned around, she'd gone. She must have slipped out through the door when I wasn't looking. And then the storm came but, my gosh, it really is her."

Whoosh!

I see a flash of light. The photographer takes a step back.

"So, you're really retiring Smoky, huh?" the photographer asks Bill.

"Yep. This is it, as they say. We've been ten years at the top, but I think it's time now. You know what they say about getting out while the going's good. Who'd've thought that meeting this little mite back in Nazdab would have led to all this?" Bill smiles and picks me up. We leave the offices of the *Cleveland Plain Dealer*.

Since then, I've stayed put in Bill and Margie's house. Their

---

[71] I have used artistic licence here, though who knows what thoughts went through Smoky's head at that time… See Epilogue.

home, my home. I've sat and watched and played with Bill and Margie's puppy people. I've watched them sit up and crawl, stand and talk. I've watched them be loved and cared for, just like I've felt loved and cared for. I think of Petrilak, I think of helping Gapp, I even think of horrible Downey. Then I think of — no, I see — Major. He's caught up in this whirlwind too, just like Topper and Bobby. This warm, comforting whirlwind that is wrapping itself around me.

I can still see and feel everything. Running through the pipe, hiding in the hole, jumping into the bag. I am moving and not moving. The whirlwind is taking me away. It's taking me past the hole where I was shaking and frightened, past being with Grace. "Let's call her Christmas!" Grace smiles and hugs the man she is with.

I see Downey again, calling me a jungle rat and throwing me into the truck. I see Dare picking me up — "there you are, Smokums" — and watch as my hair falls all around me, blowing away in the wind. Bill is showing me around the camp. "I'm not even supposed to be here." But what would have happened if you weren't there, Bill? What would have happened to me? To us?

"He's not a boy. She's a girl. And she's a Yorkie too."

I fall out of the tree, straight into the arms of a GI with wet eyes, sitting in a chair on wheels. I am on a ship with Duke, in a plane with Major. "Sniff. What's your name?"

"I'm the Champion mascot of the SWPA."

"You're a war dog. That's what you are."

I see Topper and Bobby again. They're standing there, waiting…

I'm a mummy dog!

The whirlwind slows right down. It wraps around me like my

favourite blanket. It's getting even darker. The whirlwind is getting tighter, the hurt in my tummy throbs and throbs. I can't see! I must have my blindfold on. I must be on the wires! I step out. I don't fall. I hear the audience clap and cheer. Bill faces them and bends forward. I stand on my back legs and yip and yip. We both take a step back. The stage curtain closes in front of us, the sound of the roaring crowd rushes through me. I can hear them chanting, they're all calling my name, my name, my name...

I am a curled-up tree root, a table where the GIs eat and feed me scraps of food, the helmet I jump into all dirty and jump out of all wet and clean, the stepladder that I climb to run across the wires. I am Bill stretched out on the ground with his arms outstretched. Happy, happy, happy.

I know what they all mean now. What everything means. In darkness there is light, in a strange land there is home and, above all, in senseless war and fear, in loss and death, there is friendship and hope, warmth and love.

My eyes close.

"We did it Smoky. It's over, it's over. Time to go home."

# Epilogue

"Smoky! Smoky! Nooo…" Bill wailed. On February 21, 1957, he returned home to find his beautiful little dog was no longer with him. A strong man, he was unable to hold back the tears.

The following day, Bill, Margie and their children drove to the Cleveland Metropark, armed with a shovel, pick and Smoky's remains in a shoe box. Often called the Emerald Necklace, the park is a beautiful 21,000 acres of forests, rivers, trails, fishing spots and valleys. Bill's family made a grim procession, traipsing across a gorge and along bridle paths, looking for one particular tree.

Margie and Bill had first biked there together seventeen years earlier and the trunk of what they now called "Our Tree" still showed the evidence — a carved heart, with the initials B.W. above M.R., along with '40. It seemed a fitting spot for Smoky's final place of rest.

One can only imagine Bill's grief as he set about digging a grave for his friend and companion of so many years. Smoky had kept him going, raised his spirits through the hardships of war and the treacherous jungle environment, and been his work colleague and friend both in Hollywood and on television. She had been his light, his life, his love for thirteen years, always at his side, always trusting and happy, showering him with her unique brand of playful, Yorkie affection.

Choking back his grief, Bill finally laid Smoky to rest, covering her box with dirt and marking the site with stones. Eyes brimming with tears, his children stood in silence and watched. The family sadly tramped back to their car.

After Smoky's death, Bill was contacted by Grace Heidenreich, who had seen Smoky's obituary. A lieutenant assigned to a field hospital in Dobodura, Papua New Guinea early in 1944, she had lost a valuable Yorkshire Terrier she called Christmas when it ran off one day. Her little dog had not been seen since. Very few Yorkies were bred during WWII, Smoky and Christmas looked identical, Smoky had reacted strongly to Bill every time he said the word "Christmas." They concluded that someone had found the little dog wandering around and taken her to Nazdab. Christmas and Smoky were one and the same.

Smoky's worldwide fame did not stop with her death. She has inspired numerous memorials nationally, been awarded further medals and been the subject of several television shows and documentaries.

On December 11, 2015, the Purple Cross Award, Australia's RSPCA's[72] most prestigious animal bravery award, was bestowed upon Smoky and presented to Bill in Ohio. She continues to appear regularly in the press and, with talk of a potential movie in the pipeline, it looks as if this little bundle of heroic and therapeutic fun will continue to be a star for many years to come.

Always chirpy and cheerful, tongue panting, eyes glistening, she never let life or circumstances daunt her little spirit, despite having lost two pups of her own. A reminder of the joy animals can bring, Smoky was not just an inspirational war hero and the first therapy dog on record, but one of the greatest trained dogs of her time.

---

[72] Royal Society for the Prevention of Cruelty to Animals.

# Contact the author

If you have enjoyed reading *Smoky: How a Tiny Yorkshire Terrier Became a World War II American Army Hero, Therapy Dog and Hollywood Star,* I would be extremely grateful if you could leave a review on Amazon.

I hope you will also enjoy the first book in my Animal Heroes series, *Simon Ships Out, How a Brave, Stray Cat Became a Worldwide Hero,* which is available on Amazon in versions for adults, children and toddlers.

I'd also love to hear your comments and am happy to answer any questions you may have, so do please get in touch with me by:

- emailing me via my website www.JackyDonovan.com

- following me on twitter - @HeroicCats

If you enjoy memoirs, I recommend you pop over to friendly Facebook group, We Love Memoirs, to chat with me and other authors there. www.facebook.com/groups/welovememoirs

I look forward to hearing from you.

Jacky Donovan

# Acknowledgements

Thanks to everyone who helped me put Smoky's story into words, enabling me to give a dog's perspective on life for these American troops during World War II. Your suggestions were invaluable in shaping the book into its final format, thank you.

I'm extremely grateful to Yoana Toteva, whose wonderful illustrations of the original photographs of Smoky help bring the story to life. Yoana's persistence toward making the images as accurate as possible showed the same dogged determination of Smoky herself.

Last, but by no means least, thank you to everyone who reads my books and gives me feedback and reviews. Without you, writing wouldn't be half as much fun.

# Sources and further information

## Books

*Yorkie Doodle Dandy: A memoir* by William A. Wynne

*Beyond the Call of Duty: Heart-warming stories of canine devotion and bravery* by Isabel George

## Videos

Smoky receives a PDSA Certificate for Animal Bravery or Devotion to Duty

Smoky and the Dogs of All Wars Memorial in Cleveland

Monumental Mysteries S01E03 Smoky the Yorkie (11 min mark Bill talking)

Smoky's Story - part of a display in the waiting area of the W.W. Armistead Veterinary Medical Center

## Memorials to Smoky

1995 Columbus, Ohio — Ohio Veternary Medicine Association Animal Hall of Fame: "#1 Dog Hero"

1996 St. Louis, Missouri — AKC Museum of the Dog

2000 Hawaii — Hickham Air Force Base

2003 Knoxville, Tennessee — University of Tennessee College of Veterinary Medicine

2004 Eastlake, Ohio — Doggy Park

2005 Lakewood, Ohio — Cleveland Metroparks

2012 Brisbane, Australia — The Royal Brisbane & Women's Hospital